Journey Without End

Journey Without End

CARLO CARRETTO

Translated by Alan Neame

Earthly life
lasts the space of a day
as against
the thousand thousand
years of God.

AVE MARIA PRESS Notre Dame, Indiana 46556

Contents

Preface

In this book I speak of life without end, that is, of the life of a person who begins a journey on this earth which will flow on into the eternal life of the kingdom. In speaking of the beginning of that life, I do not put it at the moment of birth, but at its conception in the womb of the mother. Nor is there anything extraordinary about this. Simply read about the Annunciation in the gospels to call attention to that life already pulsating in Mary's womb from the moment that the Holy Spirit overshadowed her. And still more, when Mary, visiting her cousin Elizabeth, causes the little cousin of Jesus to leap for joy. John is in the sixth month in his mother's womb.

Cardinal Ratzinger, in his famous document on the origin and development of life, speaks of this beginning in clear and simple words, giving to the embryo its true value and urging respect for sacred things. Yes! Human life is born at its conception and never ends, even if death occurs in the first months, making a tomb of the mother's womb, and/or if human malice does violence to that young life.

The theme of the aborted child imposed itself on me without my willing it, but this did not displease me, given the timeliness of the topic. It is my hope to be able to say a word of faith and of human sweetness on so bitter a subject. But to speak of embryos and of unborn babies in the role of storyteller is not easy; in fact, it is impossible if one wants to be readable.

How can one represent an aborted child after its earthly death? At this point I asked myself: What have the authors of the sacred books done to represent the angels to us, to give a face to invisible things? They have used *signs*. In fact, the word of God is full of signs, and still more the liturgy. What did Jesus himself

7

do to help us to understand the invisible kingdom? He spoke to us in parables. Parables have the power of explaining the hidden meaning of things, of giving a face to the things we do not see, of introducing us to the truth as we meditate on Christian mysteries.

Those who have made the best use of this method are artists, especially painters, who have given a face to the invisible by filling cathedrals with celestial beings, with angels, with children's figures, with the sweetest of creatures. Have you ever seen the "Crucifixion of Jesus" painted by Giotto at Assisi? The blue vault of the heavens is filled with a profusion of wings and of celestial creatures in agony as they contemplate the sufferings of Jesus. Are the angels actually like this? Who has seen them? And yet I am not at all displeased with this attempt to describe things to me in this way. It would be difficult to find any other way.

You who are reading this book will find yourself in the presence of a multitude of angels in the cathedral — and close by, a little angel on my knee. I do hope you will not be frightened. I was not frightened; rather I was completely at ease in the midst of a vast number of unborn babies who helped me to see things with greater serenity.

Editor's note: Carlo Carretto died on October 3, 1988, at the age of 78.

Introduction
The Hills of Hope

I was lucky, I consider, to be born charged with hope. All through my life this has never diminished, sustaining me throughout my journey. And that, with the passage of time, has been a pretty long one.

Perhaps I owe this to my mother who was always singing, who really knew the meaning of joy and who was also adept at putting old worn-out things to good use for the big family she raised in poverty and fear of God.

What I know for sure is, the eldest daughter's clothes were mended, made-over and handed down to the next, who followed hard behind; and the latter never had time to complain about this since she was kept busy looking after her younger brothers; and these in their turn soon got used to relying on heaven for what would undoubtedly come by and by. And in fact, poor as we were, we never went short of anything, except such things as might have served to distract and hold our little family group back on our march to heaven, intent as we were on living that simple and absorbing adventure, untroubled by perplexing problems.

Hope guided me thus through childhood and illuminated my youth, leading me into adulthood with few incidents except those normal ones designed to teach us that we are each involved in a very mysterious and exciting adventure.

If you ask me how things turned out and I have to come down to particulars, I should say the course of my life has been marked by three stages.

The first was that of total involvement: family involvement, cultural involvement, organisational involvement. This

9

lasted until I was forty. One name sums up and is the keynote of this period: Catholic Action.

I let myself be totally absorbed in it, as is my nature.

Catholic Action led me out of a small restricted family circle into an understanding of the Church, where I experienced the deep tensions in, and discovered the divine 'us' of, the Christian community.

I owe a great deal to Catholic Action and have nothing but happy memories of it.

If we made mistakes – and we certainly did – they were due to the hurly-burly in which we lived, to our idealism, to our lack of preparation. Remember the Second Vatican Council hadn't yet taken place.

What we did, however, we did in good faith and I think the Lord has found our errors easy enough to correct.

At forty I discovered another reality and, almost without realising, found myself living the stupendous adventure of the desert.

The Sahara, for me, was the true refuge of the soul, the stupendous place of contemplation, the preferred alcove for intimacy with God.

Then came the third stage which, unwished by me, was to be as it were the synthesis of the first two.

I had known action, I had known the silence of contemplation; now God led me into a time where action and contemplation were to melt into a single reality: the Church.

The Church, truly understood, is both in the desert and in the streets. It is both in the night spent in prayer and in the painful tension of a world called to regeneration in Jesus Christ.

The Church, the true Church, is contemplative and active at once, as her founder and unique exemplar, Jesus, was contemplative and active.

So now here I am, living the third stage of my life on the hills of Spello, which let us call the hills of hope.

And with good reason.

The hills of hope are real, very beautiful hills running down from Monte Subasio to the Chiona torrent which is nearly always dry, St Francis's mountain being poor in water, though not so poor as to deny life to the lovely olive trees or to the little farms expressly created to teach by the effort and hardship involved in working them what a hard life Jesus must have lived in Nazareth.

Among these olive trees, by God's unforeseen design, have sprung up some twenty prayerful hermitages restored from the tumbledown homes of country folk who have now migrated to nearby Spello. Spello itself was originally a Roman colony which the patina of the ages has now clothed in an incomparably harmonious beauty.

Twenty hermitages are no small thing, a matter indeed for discreet and loving pride, faithful to the luminous tradition of Francis of Assisi who, in this way of life between solitude and street, found the spiritual equilibrium for a life that was to reinvigorate the so-called monasticism of the West.

Benedict, who was born a few tens of kilometres from here, at Norcia to be precise, represents the other solid pillar of Italian spirituality in the centuries called 'past' though not as past as all that, since the force of their values and the dynamism of their love are still active today.

Indeed Francis with his twin tendencies, the one to the hermit-life and the other to running the streets proclaiming the gospel, is for ever a model of the eternal equilibrium of a Church that, true to Christ's teaching, strives simultaneously to be a praying and a pilgrim church, contemplative and active. Yes, just as Jesus was.

Aware from experience of the frightful pressure the modern city exerts, hundreds of men and women come to these hermitages to pray, in search of silence, drawn by the need to discover that self-same equilibrium of Francis and Benedict in the proclamation of the Word, in the liturgy lived as joy and song and in contemplative prayer matured in silence.

And it isn't only equilibrium they find.

Often they find peace of mind, comfort in trial, progressive conversion of heart, renewal of spirit, serenity of life and courage to stay faithful to a commitment growing ever harder, sometimes to the point of heroism, in pagan times like ours.

Experience, first matured in action, then in the desert, has shown me the importance of oases of light such as this, where believers can go to live the mystery of the Church; for the Church doesn't live in the desert and, although having her roots there, must have a place to welcome those who come in from the world bearing all the wounds the world can inflict and who, in the course of the daily solitary march, have constant need of renewal if they are to remain faithful to the Absolute.

I can assure you not a day passes without someone turning up in search of what he or she needs and cannot do without: I mean the Church, the community, the 'us' willed by God himself to support the loneliness of the individual.

Today it's the turn of a woman in her forties.

I find her in the hermitage called Jacob.

She's praying and crying.

Her name is Lucy. I haven't seen her before.

She asks if she can have a word with me and I take her to the community's library.

We sit down.

There's a Bible on the table.

She starts crying again and I hold her hand to encourage her to talk.

It isn't hard to begin when you're unhappy and seeking guidance.

She says, 'I've just lost my baby. I had a miscarriage. I was three months pregnant and I felt so happy! I'd been wanting a baby for such a long time. My husband and I were so glad, so excited. And then this terrible thing happened. I don't know how to go on.'

I let her cry for a while and then I say, 'Why do you say you've lost it? What did you call it?'

She looks at me in bewilderment.

'What did I call it? I didn't call it anything. It hadn't got a name.'

'Why didn't it have a name?'

'Because it wasn't born then and I didn't know what to call it.'

I took Lucy into the chapel and said, 'What would you have called it?'

'If it had been a boy I'd have called it Francis. Clare, if it had been a girl.'

'Which would you have liked?'

'I'd have liked Clare. I've got two boys already, Dominic who's seven and Stephen who's four.'

'Very well,' I said cheerfully, 'let it be Clare. You now have a little girl called Clare.'

'But she was never born!'

'What do you mean, not born? Of course she's born! It may seem to you she died in your womb at three months, but the fact is she's alive and living still. You're Clare's mother. You've got three children: Dominic, Stephen and Clare.'

'But I couldn't get her baptised. I don't know where she is.'

Gently I stroked her hair.

She looked at me and said, 'Where will she be? How am I to imagine her?'

'Think to yourself she's with God, in that state of existence with God we call heaven, paradise; and think to yourself that she's alive and happy. You have a living, happy child.'

'But I couldn't get her baptised! I've been told she's in limbo now. Limbo's where unbaptised babies go.'

'But you know, besides the baptism of water which you didn't get the chance of giving her, certainly through no fault of your own, there's the baptism of desire and the baptism of blood, which you have more than conferred on her with your tears and, I think, your heart's blood too.

'You mustn't entertain such silly, illogical notions, the absurdities – not to put too fine a point on it – of a legalistic past often tainted with superstition.

'Lucy, can you imagine it?

'A God, that very one who made heaven and earth and each of us, who is pleased to consign your baby to some dark, far-away place out of your reach for the sole reason that it didn't have a few drops of water poured on its head.

'If he were a God like this I shouldn't hesitate to say to him, due caution notwithstanding, "If that's how it is, I shan't be coming with you. You frighten me with your unjust, loveless law."

'What about you, Lucy?'

Lucy looked at me and smiled.

She grasped the point: she had to free herself from a religious culture bound more to superstition than to the Word, more to an ancestral culture than to experience of God.

Her sufferings were being caused by mindless taboos from the past or, worse, by someone's more or less religiously motivated obsession with creating an all-embracing system.

'Don't worry, Lucy.

'Remember you have your Clare, you have her alive and will see her again one day.

'You know, the conversation we've had today makes me feel I want to write a book.

'Writing books is an old habit of mine which I haven't yet managed to break, and each time I make the same excuse: Be patient with me, this will be the last.

'In this book, which I shall call *Journey Without End*, I shall try to tell you what I think about unborn children, which in point of fact is the same as I think about children who *are* born.

'Lucy, it's the same.

'Would you like to know something extraordinarily beautiful and, for some people, quite new?

'We are eternal.

'Life is eternal, Lucy!

'"Life is changed, not taken away," says the liturgy of the dead – they aren't dead since God himself gives us life and the life he gives is eternal.

'Believe, Lucy!

'Believe!

'When we are born, when we are conceived in our mother's

womb, God gives us life, which is eternal because he is eternal.

'If you were to take a one-day-old foetus and put it in poison or have it squashed under a train or take it to pieces, you would achieve nothing, you wouldn't succeed in taking its life away, for that is eternal and able to escape any death you care to devise from the moment it comes from God who is eternal.

'Now I want to tell you the story of the unborn and you must pray to your Clare to help me find the appropriate words.

'Above all, I want to find joyous ones capable of bringing comfort to thousands and thousands of mothers.

'I want to make everyone feel the joy of having thousands and thousands of brothers and sisters, of giving them lovely ringing names and letting them hear the sound of your voice as you proclaim your faith.

'I want to see these hills of hope swarming with life, populated by an immense choir of angels, archangels, cherubim and seraphim, endlessly singing, "Holy, Holy, Holy is the Lord!"

'Do you like the idea, Lucy?

'You see, there's only one difference between us and these angels that we have any cause to cry about.

'They have got there before us.

'They already know how to love, while we still don't.

'They have made fewer blunders.

'They are free.

'They are happy.'

In my spate of words I hadn't noticed Lucy was on her knees and was praying again.

You may be sure she was praying to her new-found Clare fluttering round her in the Jacob hermitage set on the hills of hope.

1

And God Created Heaven and Earth . . . and Me

And now let us set out.

We shall follow the foot-marks God has left on the ground and substance of our faith.

These foot-marks aren't disproportionate to the size of our shoes, of our sandals.

God doesn't get a kick out of asking disproportionate achievement of us.

In the course of my own journey I've observed that usually he adapts his light to our eyes.

All said and done, the faith God requires of us is reasonable, simple and straightforward.

He reveals himself a little at a time, like a father teaching a son his trade – step by step.

Normally the course we run to reach God is the same one God runs to meet us.

The meeting takes place about half-way and the reason for this is a simple one.

God doesn't want to work harder than he needs and wants to train us as children, not as slaves.

Brother, sister, listen to this parable. It's a true dream-parable about a dream without an end.

In the beginning God created heaven and earth.
Now the earth was a formless void,
there was darkness over the deep,
with a divine wind sweeping over the waters.

God said, 'Let there be light,' and there was light.
God saw that light was good,
And God divided light from darkness.
God called light 'day', and darkness he called 'night'.
Evening came and morning came: the first day.

The dream vision then proceeds, expanding in an astonishing
design.

God said,
'Let there be a vault through the middle of the waters
to divide the waters in two.'
And so it was.
God made the vault, and it divided the waters
under the vault from the waters above the vault.
God called the vault 'heaven'.
Evening came and morning came: the second day.

And God said,
'Let the waters under heaven
come together into a single mass,
and let dry land appear.'
And so it was.
God called the dry land 'earth'
and the mass of waters 'seas'.
And God saw that it was good.

And God said,
'Let the earth produce vegetation:
seed-bearing plants and fruit-trees
bearing fruit with their seed inside,
each corresponding to its own species.'
And so it was: the earth produced vegetation:
the seed-bearing plants
and the fruit-trees with seeds inside,
each corresponding to its own species.
God saw that it was good.
Evening came and morning came: the third day.

God said,

'Let there be lights in the vault of heaven
to divide day from night,
and let them indicate
festivals, days and years.
Let them be lights in the vault of heaven
to shine on the earth.'
And so it was.
God made the two great lights:
the greater light to govern the day,
the smaller light to govern the night,
and the stars.
God set them in the vault of heaven
to shine on the earth,
to govern day and night
and to divide light from darkness.
God saw that it was good.
Evening came and morning came: the fourth day.

God said,
'Let the waters swarm with living creatures
and let birds wing their way above the earth
across the vault of heaven.'
And so it was.
God created great sea-monsters
and all the creatures that glide
and team in the waters
in their own species,
and winged birds in their own species.
God saw that it was good.
God blessed them, saying, 'Be fruitful, multiply,
and fill the waters of the seas;
and let the birds multiply on land.'
Evening came and morning came: the fifth day.

God said,
'Let the earth produce every kind of living creature
in its own species: livestock, creeping things
and wild animals of all kinds.' And so it was.
God made wild animals in their own species,

and livestock in theirs, and every creature that crawls
along the earth in its own species.
God saw that it was good.

And God said,
'Let us make man in our own image,
in the likeness of ourselves,
and let them be masters of the fish of the sea,
the birds of heaven, the livestock, all the wild animals
and all the creatures that creep along the ground.'
God created man in the image of himself,
in the image of God he created him,
male and female he created them . . .

God saw all he had made
and indeed it was very good.
Evening came and morning came: the sixth day. (Gen. 1)

And at this point, between that evening – the sixth – and
next morning, I too was born.

I don't remember much about it, since I was very small
and had my eyes shut.

I was to understand about it later.

But my ears were open and so, particularly, was my
mouth, and I found no difficulty in repeating that same
phrase God himself had uttered, since I already knew it by
heart.

I too said enthusiastically, 'It was very good.'

And I repeated it seven times, just as it's repeated seven
times to the praise of God in the creation story:

It was very good.
It was very good.
It was very good.
It was very good.
It was very good.
It was very good.
It was very good.

This was the earliest liturgy of my life and my church was
my mother's womb.

There's no need for me to explain the facts of life to you and how this all came about.

You're better informed than the silly-billies of my day who imagined babies were born under a big barrel or were brought from far-away places by the stork.

Even if my mother's belly did look like a big round barrel to the stork's inquisitive eye, everything took place very simply, very intimately.

So intimately as to be one integral event.

Later, when I was grown up, that sublime moment of love was best summed up for me in the phrase once used by my elder brother Jesus, who meant what he said, having seen all from the beginning: 'You in me, I in you, so that we may be one' (cf. John 17:23,26).

Truly wonderful!

What an exchange of joy under the blankets!

As though God himself had undertaken to let my father and mother feel the same joy he had felt in the explosive instant of creation, when from irrational chaos he brought forth life, harmony, beauty, being.

It's a pity there isn't a theology of pleasure, and that the best things in life should have been made ugly by that monstrously stupid being, often passing himself off as a theologian, known as human.

Always dissatisfied from the word go, always sullen, always pessimistic. Totally unable to appreciate how wonderful it all was and how delighted God himself was with it.

But the fact of the matter is, he had the Evil One forever at his elbow, forever envious.

Very envious; what's more, very wicked.

Wasn't it wicked to think giving life to a lovely baby was sinful?

Wasn't it wicked to suggest some trick or other to prevent my father's and mother's bodies being totally united?

Wasn't it wicked to disrupt that moment with worries about whether there would be enough to feed me when I arrived to swell the number of mouths in the world – at the

very moment when God's fertility was showing there was
no need to worry?

Wasn't it wicked to soil the sheet by scattering the seed,
as Onan did to avoid giving his wife children, thereby giving
displeasure to God?

Great displeasure.

Great displeasure.

O night of fire when love takes cognisance of the love that
is God himself!

O night of fire when the happiness of God becomes the
happiness of human beings!

O night of fire when fear is overcome by courage for the
divine adventure!

O night of fire when the human race was created in the
image and likeness of God: his child, begotten of his loins,
not 'made' as you might make a picture or some other object!

O night of joy, purest joy, alone charged with the power
to increase hope and make life's hardships tolerable!

O night of glory transforming the act of love into that
most stupendous of all signs to explain the union of Yahweh
and Israel his bride!

But that's not all.

At that moment of conception God who is love, for fear
lest anyone should get rid of that stupendous gift which a
child is (and it wouldn't be difficult), clothes it with
immortality.

'You are my child for ever.

'You are mine for ever,' he tells me.

Can you conceive of God behaving otherwise?

Can you conceive of the opposite, for instance?

Can you imagine the God of life saying, 'I shall hang on
to this scrap of life for a little while, I'll have a bit of fun
with it and then not think about it any more, leave it to
itself, to non-life, to death'?

I can't.

And if indeed he were a God who made sport of my
littleness, I should be the one to leave him to himself and

get in first, screaming with every fibre, 'You aren't God. You're only his wicked shadow.'

No, brothers. No, sisters. Never forget it: we are eternal.

It's a matter of logic.

Love wills it thus.

From the instant we're programmed by God and conceived in our mother's womb, we're distinct individuals, individually named, each with our papers in order; and the divine Person watching over us, who has loved us from eternity, cannot help but go on loving and willing our wellbeing, willing us all that is good.

No one has the power to cancel the eternal life given to me by God, no one.

'Don't fool yourself,' you will retort.

'Look what goes on. This foetus, for instance. Its weakness puts it at everyone's mercy.

'Medical technique can make it disintegrate, can force it out of the maternal uterus with a little spoon, reduce it to little pieces or whisk it up to nothing in a trice so that it won't be so upsetting to look at.

'How can you say nobody can harm it?'

No, no, brothers and sisters.

No.

Not even the doctor, for all his techniques, can harm the life that is eternal.

You can change it but you can't destroy it.

There is no more death.

You can't die now, since God gave you eternal life at your conception.

God was incredibly happy that day, and his design was clear and precise.

From now on you can throw yourself out of the window.

You'll leave your blood-stained body on the pavement but you'll go on living in spite of your death-wish.

You can walk into a furnace and be burnt to ashes.

You'll change nothing of your supernatural essence and still live on, though in a different mode.

If we only knew how to get this prophecy of life across!

What new light would flood our existence.

What certitude would spring from this hope.
What endless praises leap forth to our God.

On that night, an adventure without end began for me.

So listen, since the same thing has happened to you; for you too, the journey that has no end has begun.

2

The Hospital Rubbish Bin

The journey will go on; no one can interrupt it even if it passes through the 'dark valley', as Psalm 23 has it.

God is there in the dark valley too.

God is everywhere and his presence is ever-present.

'Even though the mountains collapsed and plunged into the abyss, I shouldn't be frightened, since you are with me' (cf. Ps. 46:3).

The evil which is in the world cannot change the course of things. God is ever victorious.

With loving eye God watches over his child even when dumped in a hospital rubbish bin.

As they have done here.

Don't be shocked when I tell you this story.

Rather recognise God's victory in it.

Abortion has now gained enormous ground everywhere. We should do better to regard it not only as a breach of the law but as a sin.

We should do better to entertain a little hope.

By our attitude to abortion we can assess our own degree of faith.

Don't ask me where I was.

I've travelled a lot in my life.

What I'm about to tell you could have happened in New York, Tokyo or Rio.

It could have taken place quite near here, in Turin, for instance, or down the road in Foligno.

Don't ask me for details; I'm no policeman.

All I know, it was hard going with my bad leg. As always, I needed somebody to lean on.

That's how it was.

Yes, that was the way of it.

Anyhow, I was near a hospital. Chief among my many impressions was the acrid smell of disinfectant.

I came out of a church where I had been spending the night praying with friends, adoring the Eucharist, as we say in religious jargon.

It was pretty cold and a colourless light announced the coming of dawn on the hills lying ahead of me at the bottom of an avenue of plane trees.

On the right hand side of the street were some railings and, among a number of vehicles parked overnight in the open, I saw the grey mass of a big metal rubbish skip with two rotating lids.

One of my friends, a hospital orderly, took me by the arm. He was fairly old and I'd known him a long time: a very lively chap, interested in what went on around him.

'Come over here,' he said. 'I want to show you what goes on these days. It's sad, very sad, but that's the way it is and there's nothing we can do about it but pray and, on occasion, weep.'

He went over to the rubbish skip and opened the lid as though all too familiar with the problem.

He took out a pocket torch and, using the walking-stick I always carry, began turning over the contents of the skip while I leaned against the truck on the back of which it was loaded.

It was coldly metallic to the touch.

'Look,' said my friend, 'here we are. I want you to take a look at this.

'Look here.

'These are the abortions carried out in the hospital.'

I looked and by the dim light of the torch, amid the bloodstained, dirty bandages, I saw a scrap of smooth pink flesh curled up in the characteristic position of a human foetus.

Naturally it was quite still and even though we were forced

by curiosity to look for any possible sign of life, I didn't detect any.

I tried to meet my friend's eye.

'You see,' he went on sadly, 'you now see what a point our dehumanised, murderous society has reached.'

I couldn't bring myself to answer, overwhelmed as I was by the unexpected horror of evil masquerading as commonplace, carefree normality.

The hospital orderly closed the lid and we walked very slowly away in silence.

In the avenue was a tiny public garden where we went and sat on a newly varnished park-seat which left stripes on our trousers: another symbol of things ill done, without any sense of responsibility, in society today.

'What would you say to praying a little, brother?

'I've just had an idea.

'Take out your torch.

'I want to read you a passage from Ezekiel.

'It applies exactly to our case; we aren't the first to see what we have seen this morning.'

I took the Bible out of my bag and looked for the passage in the prophet's sixteenth chapter.

It was the exact description of what other people too had seen but set in a somewhat different context and applying to us from a night long ago.

The night God came to the rescue.

This is what it said, and it said it about me, you and everyone.

At your birth, the very day you were born,
there was no one to cut your navel-string
or wash you in water to clean you,
or rub you with salt,
or wrap you in swaddling clothes.
No one looked at you with pity enough
to do any of these things
out of sympathy for you.
You were exposed in the open fields
in your own dirt,

the day you were born.
I saw you kicking on the ground in your blood
as I was passing, and I said to you,
'Live – and grow
like the grass of the fields!' (Ezek. 16:4–6)

Live, live, live! And grow like the grass of the fields . . .
I kept on repeating Ezekiel's words.
There was a great silence all around us.
My companion had dropped off to sleep.
Leaning against my shoulder, he never moved, whether from weariness or perhaps from sadness.
Dawn began to tint the sky between the branches of the plane trees.
I didn't feel like going to sleep.
I wasn't a hospital orderly and I was too upset by what I'd seen.
It was the first time – for me.
Live, live, live! I kept praying in a sort of litany of hope.
I kept my eyes half-closed and, the violent emotions to which I had been subjected notwithstanding, peace filled my soul and I felt myself enfolded in the sweet presence of my God.
I lost the sense of time and place, as happens to me when, absorbed in prayer, I succeed in going beyond things.
Slowly I became aware of a very small angel smiling at me on my knee.
It seemed to me to be moving its lips and repeating the word 'Live!' in time with me as though we were saying the rosary together.
I smiled back but made very sure not to move in case it disappeared.
But no, it stayed there without moving as I gradually perceived the resemblance between the foetus seen in the hospital rubbish skip and the little cherub standing on my knee and praying with me the while that one word: Live, live, live!
This isn't something of this world, I thought, perhaps I'm dreaming.

But I wasn't bothered.

I felt happy and that was enough.

Besides, can't you live on dreams?

How can you tell dream from reality?

And suppose reality were no more than a dream?

Better still, suppose the dream were indeed reality . . .

Be that as it may, as I sat with my legs crossed, I distinctly saw a very small angel on my knee and that very small angel was undoubtedly the embryo I'd seen in the hospital rubbish skip.

We fell to chatting like old friends and what immediately struck me was how joyful it was.

A full, conscious, mature, irrepressible joy.

I kept saying how abominably it had been treated but this only made it laugh, as though what had happened was something quite trivial.

Something else was much more important.

'Yes, I feel sorry for my mother.

'She's the one who's suffering.

'My father's an unthinking kind of man and he too will suffer one day when he finds himself quite on his own.

'I was a nuisance to the two of them, so they got rid of me.

'Still, you must allow them this: they gave me life and that's no small matter.

'You know what St Augustine says: that the benefit of life is so great that hell would be preferable to non-existence.

'He may overstate the case a bit, but he's trying to explain things as they are and show how important life is.

'Life is indeed important since it's eternal and leads to the vision of the Absolute of God.

'I'm grateful to my father and mother in spite of what they've done.

'I don't feel any desire to judge them.

'The fact is, even though I wasn't wanted, I've managed to come into existence.

'I'm alive. Alive for ever, you realise.

'That's no small matter.

'As far as I know, my father's a poor man and rather irresponsible.

'You can't blame him, considering what he sees every day on TV.

'My mother?

'Yes, I'm sorry about my mother but one day, when we meet again in the kingdom, we shall be able to make it up.

'By then she'll have understood, especially when she's done a stint of crying.

'Meanwhile I'm alive.

'I'm alive.

'I'm alive.

'I'm alive.

'I've been through the worst of it, I'm alive.

'Imagine, I'll still be alive millions and millions of years from now. How wonderful to be able to contemplate the face of our real father, God.

'One thing's for sure: human beings are poor tools.

'They cause such a lot of suffering.

'I think people who can bring themselves to get rid of a defenceless baby must make God suffer too.

'I don't feel any rancour towards them, but . . .

'But they make me very unhappy.

'In all sincerity I say of them what Jesus said on the cross: "Father forgive them, they don't know what they're doing" (Luke 23:34).

'How distant human beings are from the truth of things.

'They could be so happy, but instead, you might think, they go out of their way to injure themselves.'

'So where are you going next?' I asked my very small angel as he still stood balancing on my knee.

'Where am I going?

'I'm going to set out on my journey like everyone else.

'I'm not alone, you know.

'If you only knew what a lot of us there are! We can't all fit inside the cathedral, there are such a lot of us.

'And we're all so happy.

'We're setting out on our journey with a few months

in hand and we're fully aware, what's more, of receiving preferential treatment.

'God's taken note of the wrong done us when the peaceful life we were leading in our mother's womb was so brutally cut short.

'That's what you'd expect.

'God is God and knows how to draw good out of evil.

'God is invincible.

'He is love, and love is the greatest reality that exists.

'Love conquers all, explains all, knows all.

'It would be a poor look-out for us if it weren't for love.

'Neither you nor I would be alive; no one would.

'Through love God created us and living with him is endless holiday.

'Now it's up to us to make an effort.

'We've already been told we shall need to suffer, pay, journey, purify ourselves.

'We've already been told there'll be choices to be made, ties to be cut.

'We've got to mature, got to grow in him, got to search for him, often in the dark.

'In a word, it's the same journey we're making, you and I, and no doubt we shall meet quite often, even if we don't always find it easy to recognise one another.

'I've already seen the job that's entrusted to me.

'My aim's to be a good child.

'You won't have to do this so much, but my task will be to pray for my parents.

'They need it and I shall have to help them all I can.

'They too, like me, will have to cross the desert, come out of Egypt, journey in faith and learn how to pray.

'They are eternal too.

'My guess is, since they're rather thoughtless, God will reclaim them by sorrow.

'There's no resisting God.

'Besides, he understands and knows what must be done. He's God!'

At this point I felt the very small angel stir as though getting ready to fly away.

'Where are you off to now?' I asked.

'I'm going to the cathedral.

'I have to recite morning prayer with all the ones who were got rid of last night.

'What a lot of us there are!

'We shall fill the building.'

'Tell me one more thing: what's your name, what are you called?'

'Unborn, for the time being.

'It's a generic name while I wait for the one my mother may give me, should she remember me.

'And she will remember, you see.'

And suddenly he wasn't there any more.

He had flown away on his tiny wings.

I touched the knee he'd been standing on.

It was still warm.

I lifted my hand to my face and smelt a wonderful perfume on my fingers.

This helped me forget the stench of the disinfectant.

Sunrise couldn't be far off now.

My friend the orderly woke up in a fright like a guilty man.

He apologised profusely.

But he little knew what a service he'd done me.

Slowly, slowly we resumed our walk, I leaning on him, he silent and abstracted.

3

Starting From Scratch

The journey now comes to a halt in a fine cathedral.

I hope you're not going to be shocked. Remember this is a way-out story about a gathering of cherubim.

But it isn't merely a story. You yourself may be the judge of that.

If you know your Bible, you can even look up the reference.

It's about the famous assembly at Shechem that Joshua and his surviving followers held on first entering the Promised Land.

It's in the twenty-fourth chapter of the Book of Joshua, which says a number of important things but, most important of all, enthusiastically records their decision never again to betray the Lord.

It deals with choice, definitive choice.

Without which we end up for ever midway between yes and no.

And so our moral standards, if not dictated by firm and conscious faith, grow weaker and weaker the further we go, to the scandal of our fellow-pilgrims.

The little cherub's parting words as he left my knee that morning gradually sank in and aroused my curiosity accordingly.

He'd said, 'Now I'm off to the cathedral to pray . . . if you could only see what a lot of us there are!'

I spent the day in thought but by the evening couldn't resist going back into town.

I gave the sacristan a handsome tip and had myself locked inside the cathedral on the pretext, though it wasn't only a pretext, of spending some time in prayer.

It wasn't the first time I'd thought up a ruse like this, and the sacristan, who was pious and devout, saw no obstacle to satisfying my wishes.

He merely told me to keep an eye on the lamps, to call him if anything untoward happened and to pray a little for him too, since he suffered from asthma and had a son out of work to add to his worries.

Having promised to do everything he wanted I went and settled down in the massive wooden choir of the cathedral, built in the Gothic style, uncommonly lovely and harmonious.

I chose a stall well-placed for me to see the lamp burning in front of the Blessed Sacrament and, given the many distracting experiences of the day, began to pray as well as I could. I felt at peace and assured myself I shouldn't see anything odd.

However . . .

It was already dark when I began to hear a restrained whispering here and there and mysterious, though far from unpleasant, little voices.

They were coming from all directions but I felt quite calm.

Then, I don't know how it came about but I found myself on the other side of things, where I love to be whenever I enter the living substance of faith, of real faith.

The cathedral lamps had all gone out; instead, a strange diffused light began to appear, seemingly coming from far, far away and yet having its source extremely near.

When the light grew sufficiently strong I saw an incomparable sight; gradually more and more details became clear.

The cathedral I had supposed empty was crowded – and you won't believe this – with angels, archangels, cherubim and seraphim of every size.

Each had human, absolutely human, form.

They all had this in common.

Every scrap of space was taken up.

They were on the choir stalls, on the altars, on the picture-frames, on the lamp-holders, on the cornices.

It seemed the dome was alive with ultra-lively birds: the youngest and most restless ones, I suppose.

They all gave off lights and the dominant colours were gold and deep blue – what Umbrian painters called 'Giotto blue'.

It was like a very meeting-place of heaven and what astounded me was their extraordinary variety.

There wasn't a single angel that looked like another.

All had individual personality, individual build, faces rich in character.

Their voices were enthralling, not in the least discordant, and even though their number might have favoured uproar and confusion, everything took place in perfect calm.

Lowering my gaze, I was surprised to see the same personage on my knee as had straddled it that morning, now looking happily at me as though delighted I had come.

We seemed to be friends of long-standing and I think he had put in a word with the All Highest to allow me to attend the great assembly.

For the assembly was really enormous.

I would never have believed there could be so many still-born children in the world, whether aborted or otherwise.

If I had seen so many in the particular city where I was, who could tell about elsewhere!

There was every type and kind and each displayed the signs of an individual martyrdom.

There were those that had been sucked out of their mother's womb, others that had been poisoned with herbal potions, others that had been stabbed to death with hat-pins, others that had been reduced to atoms.

It looked as though one of the principal aims of the medical profession had been to find the fastest and most efficient method, but the end was always the same: to get rid of the intruder.

I observed with delight that the essence of human individuality didn't reside in the body manifesting it, but in a personal light expressing it.

Certainly there you couldn't have distinguished body from soul.

The situation was quite different.

A truly new unity, different from the ones we know about.

I asked my little friend, now ensconced on my knee, if he could explain the nature of the lovely light enveloping them all, since it was something totally novel to me.

'It's eternal life,' was his confident reply.

'You see,' he went on joyfully, 'we're born at the moment we're conceived. Born in that instant when human love between our father and mother is unleashed like a hurricane of life, to fulfil God's design of making one single entity out of two: for such is the law of love.

'And God in person at that instant intervenes to invest what is born of human love with the light you mention.

'The light is eternal life and no one can kill it.

'It's eternal.

'You understand how important this is?

'It's the greatest gift God has in his power to bestow.

'It is itself absolute.

'So it's futile to tax one's brains trying to work out whether we begin being human at two months or at six . . .

'Useless to speculate over when God puts the soul into the body.

'These are the empty triflings of under-employed theologians.

'God who is love by love created us in his own image and likeness; he created us by means of that act of human love which, limited, soiled, sick, immature, self-centred as it may be, is still an act of love none the less, and which, as you know from the Bible, is the perfect image of the covenant between God and the human race, between Yahweh and Israel, as Hosea, Ezekiel, Isaiah and the other prophets all teach us.

'From that instant of conception which, whether you like it or not, is an act of love, the human entity is the child of God; it is immortal and death cannot touch it.

'Strange indeed the God who programmed a child (and,

believe me, whoever is born has been programmed by God) and then abandoned it to death and thought no more of it.

'He wouldn't be a God at all; we should have every justification for steering clear of anyone like that.

'But this isn't how it works.

'Human beings are immortal because God, our Father, is immortal.

'Of course, we have a journey to make.

'A long, painful, single-minded journey.

'Since we have to reach a point when we are capable of loving.

'Not in the way our parents loved when they conceived us without the capacity to welcome us, but of loving maturely, consciously, genuinely.

'We have to reach the stage of loving like Jesus on the cross, a true death to self, a total self-giving.

'It's a journey.

'A journey beginning with an exodus, as Scripture says: a conscious exodus from the slavery of Egypt, that is to say, from sin.

'A journey requiring strength to cross the desert, advancing through the absolute darkness of non-existence, which is the true death, to win the victory over our own pride, sensuality and selfishness.

'It isn't an easy one to make.

'And here's something very important that must be said at the outset if you're to grasp the direction and meaning of this journey.

'The human journey isn't accomplished on this earth only, as many people are convinced.

'So convinced, they regard the graveyard as the absolute term of the march and the end of everything.

'That's a fundamental error.

'For in fact the graveyard is no more than a wardrobe in which, as we would an old suit, we lay aside the first and by no means most important sign of our existence.

'Death – from the instant we're eternal – exists only as a sign.

'The horrid wardrobe is there to warn us of important

matters, to make us think a bit and then resume the march, leading far beyond.

'In a word, earthly life is but the first, very short stretch of the journey to be done; it is very far from completing it.

'This is the time of "the grain of wheat that dies in the earth"; it lasts the space of a day as against the thousand thousand years of God.

'None the less it is very important since in God everything is important.

'Once earthly life is over, another period begins in different form, with different signs, although no more eternal than the first since even the first was eternal, given that its value is represented by the light investing the substance of humanity, which was bestowed by God in the beginning, at the moment of conception.

'Eternal life, true life, is that same knowledge of God, increasing in the course of our journey though never changing the nature of things.

'It is knowledge before earthly death and knowledge afterwards, although in a different reality.'

I was open-mouthed before this high-spirited little creature who spoke of matters so deep with such sagacity, and I realised that his death had not been in vain.

For he had indeed achieved the decisive transition, that passage to new life where faith, hope and charity took on new dimensions and where the vision of things was far more mature than that obtaining during the very short time he had spent in his mother's womb.

God had lost no time about it but had himself taught this baby life's true catechism.

I thought to myself: If this one talks like this and is so mature in what he says, what will it be like when the whole concourse of these beings – tiny as they are, yet clothed in eternal life and already so mature – begins its assembly?

And at that very moment the assembly began.

It reminded me of the assembly held by the people of God at Shechem, as described in the Book of Joshua, Chapter 24.

From end to end, the cathedral was astir with life and light, and the immense sufferings of all these beings murdered on the streets of the Promised Land put me in mind of the death-camps of Buchenwald and the gas-ovens of Auschwitz.

Besides, who better than this people, condemned to liquidation by the selfishness and folly of their parents, had the right to speak?

The smallest spoke up first, being, according to the gospel, the greatest.

He had settled on the central chandelier and his little voice rang out like a voice from the realms above.

He was one of the clandestinely aborted, stabbed with a hat-pin by a termagant who did things very cheap and enjoyed great confidence, especially among senior girls at high school.

'Brothers and sisters,' he said, 'the time has come to make a fresh start.

'If things go on like this, God will have to stop endowing the human race with eternal life.

'We can truly say:

When the Son of man comes,
will he find any faith on earth? (Luke 18:8).

'This is no trifling matter.

'We are the victims of an unbridled self-centredness, yet cannot accuse the guilty.

'We are not here for that.

'I cannot find it in me to accuse my mother who was desperately poor.

'I bear no grudge against her whatever and, when I think of her, I feel nothing but peace and tenderness towards her.

'We are gathered here in this cathedral to pray and above all to love those who have wronged us.

'But I would just like to say one or two things which seem appropriate, so that truth may triumph and not error.

'You all know the agenda for the meeting.

'We must be straightforward in our approach and offer a clear response to some of those questions vexing the human race, given the darkness in which they live and from which their muddleheaded logic and lack of faith will not permit them to escape.

'We must find a common thought by means of which to suggest to those brothers and sisters of ours, still at the earthly stage, those ideas that come from God: not those from human beings, theologians included, since the latter are always in danger of being ruled by moral considerations rather than by love and of attaching more importance to the act than the intention.

'The first question we have to ask is this:

'Which is better, life or death?

'Which is better, love or morality?

'Which is better, to be born or not to be born?

'I am certain how you will answer; I merely want to get a few things clear which aren't necessarily clear to Christians and which, to my mind, make the situation very much worse, complicated as it is in any case.

'In my own home, morality ruled and with it fear of hell.

'When I was programmed by God to be born and come into this world, my mother had the misfortune to discover in some bookshop or other a book about something called the Billings method which, according to the latest pundits, was far and away more accurate than the old method known as Ogino-Knaus.

'You may be hazy about the details but you know the general idea.

'How to prevent babies from being born by accident while still conforming to the rules of morality.

'I don't hold with the Billings method, I don't hold with those who exclusively study the method but neglect reading the Bible – which teaches how much God loves life and wants to propagate it and how his providence lovingly watches over each life, over every human being – and so contrive by artifice and selfishness to frustrate the programming done by God. My mother, I heard it said at home, was very regular in her cycles and always had her temperature just right.

'In a word then, with this well-tried method, I should never have come into the world at all.

'Morality would have been intact, but the divine programming designed to bring me to birth would have been mocked by my mother's scheming and selfishness.

'As luck would have it, she got her sums wrong and I was born all the same; yes, I was born.

'I was lucky enough to be born, though entirely by mistake, with the full consecration of morality.

'You can see these methods aren't any good, since they get believers used to paying more attention to morality than to love, more to the act than to the intention.

'In a word, the methods make them self-centred.

'Wouldn't it be better to promote faith in God, the hope that he is the true Father, that there's no need to be afraid of babies, that food won't run out since God is almighty?

'And now, in passing, I want to ask you a question:

'Those of you who were conceived by mistake, raise your right hand.'

Laughter rippled through the assembly.

Raised hands were in an overwhelming majority.

Most of those present had been born by mistake.

The presiding angel then proposed a resolution to be entered in the minutes of the meeting: 'We are convinced that morality isn't enough.

'Something else is needed.

'When God programmes the birth of a baby, it's better to trust absolutely and totally in him.

'God is God and can't get his sums wrong.

'All in favour?'

Needless to say, the vote was unanimous.

It was a marvellous affair, this second Shechem.

All those little creatures who had evaded destruction in this second Buchenwald, not by any human merit but by free grace of God who had endowed them with eternal life, reaffirmed their joy, as freely responding as God's gift had been freely given, and asserting God's pre-eminence over feeble human nature.

Henceforward it wasn't to be morality that saved us but the generosity of the human heart assenting to give life as a gift of love.

No longer reliance on method, but reliance on faith and generosity in the conflicts of life.

The assembly brought its business to a close with a harmonious hymn, which echoed the oath at Shechem:

Far be it from us to desert the Lord
and to serve other gods . . .
We intend to serve the Lord
for he is our God. (Jos. 24:16,18)

Then a voice interposed, like Joshua's at Shechem:

You will not be able to serve the Lord,
since he is a holy God . . . (Jos. 24:19)
You will serve him only if you believe in life,
if you are witnesses to life . . .

Came the response like thunder:

The Lord our God is the only God we shall serve,
and we shall be witnesses to life;
his voice we shall obey. (Jos. 24:24)

I fancy this shout must have roused the sacristan, for I heard a movement over by the sacristy.

But it didn't last long and night resumed its reign.

The little ones were tired and dropped peacefully off to sleep.

4

Exodus

St John of the Cross speaks of ten degrees of love of God.

St Benedict speaks of twelve degrees of humility.

Less ambitiously, in this book I shall talk about seven stages of the journey.

Each of us does what he can.

I shall deal with the exodus from the slavery of sin represented by Egypt, with crossing the desert, by which I mean purification, with not being afraid in the dark night, with approaching the Promised Land beyond Mount Nebo, with putting all our faith in God, with attacking Jericho in the full confidence that comes from prayer, and with then launching resolutely on the final step: the cross of the risen Lord.

The whole comprises a single reality, sustained by faith, hope and love, experienced by the people of God in their quest for freedom, living-space and God.

And God himself and God alone is architect of the final victory.

Exodus is the first stage of the journey, a journey that begins at our conception and can't do otherwise than that, since life is as eternal as the eternal God who gives it.

It was while reading the works of St John of the Cross that I first discovered the inner logic of the human journey through the created world.

It's a journey that can't be arrested, having its beginning at the instant of conception and evolving through various stages to bring us to the perfection of the kingdom.

The Spanish saint describes all this with a precision and clarity that cannot fail to convince you.

But, I then began to wonder, is it the same for everyone?

Is this the ultimate meaning of existence?

Must I too reach upwards to perfection?

Just like him?

Suppose I die first?

And if my journey is cut short by death and my immaturity is obvious owing to sin, what happens then?

I shan't succeed in achieving perfection or maturity like him.

Shall I get stuck, aborted, half-way?

No.

Everyone must reach out towards fulfilment.

And if the arc of life isn't long enough, as usually it isn't, the human journey will go on through ages succeeding earthly death and lead us, through purification, to the kingdom.

In the gospel, John speaks of the grain of wheat dying in the soil to bear abundant fruit.

Exactly: the death of the grain in the soil is the first phase, the one we live down here on earth.

Then up springs a little stalk, growing longer and longer, growing until it becomes a firm support about a metre long for the ear, which develops afterwards on the tip.

The grain's death is the earthly phase; the growth of the stalk is purgatory where the journey continues, and the kingdom is the final stage, lasting without further interruption in the eternity of God.

Exodus leads us towards freedom.

It's the slowly maturing awareness of having been born enslaved to our limitations, eventually making us decide to free ourselves from all the pharaohs within that dominate us by means of sin: sin being a synthesis of the actual evil holding sway on earth.

This is no simple or easy undertaking but an extremely important one none the less, since the greatest gift God has conferred on us, second only to eternal life, is at stake: the gift of freedom.

Human beings are made to be free, human beings are made for freedom, since only in freedom can they fully express the truth and love fundamentally necessary for them.

Freedom is our glory, the soil on which we set our victorious feet, the infinite scope of our dignity as children of God.

All the while we aren't free, we can't be children, only slaves.

All the while we aren't free, we're at the mercy of hidden forces, living in chaos, in the irrationality of the inconsistent, the irrationality of death.

There are no limits to our slavery: an abyss swallowing us piecemeal.

The slavery of the senses brutalises us, the slavery of thought diminishes us, the slavery of pride distorts us.

Nothing is more monstrous than slavery, nothing more lamentable, nothing more aberrant.

The greatness of Moses lay in realising the grave effects of slavery and the importance freedom could have for the destiny of his people.

The tasty, stimulating onions (Num. 11:5) didn't count, a comfortable life didn't count; what counted was freedom, even when purchased with unheard-of sacrifices and emaciating marches through the desert.

On freedom depends our human dignity, our strength to pursue the journey to the Promised Land, the significance of the divine within us, our hope of attaining the goal.

From Moses, the true Israelite learns never to bend the knee except to Yahweh himself in the name of freedom.

The Book of Exodus tells an amazing story and highlights all those actions which lead us, little by little, to the dignity of children of God.

In Exodus we can find the reasons for our maturing so slowly, the limitations and inexperience of our childhood, tears for our sins, the joyous hymn of victory over evil.

Furthermore Exodus sums up the adult aspect of the story we're involved in, the hidden reason for our collective errors, the extenuating circumstances for our failures, the reasons for patience, the constancy of our hope.

In Exodus I can say: What I did wrong I shall not do again, and what is right, that I shall go on doing.

It becomes easy to say with Paul: 'When I was a child, I used to talk like a child and see things as a child does, and think like a child. But now I think like an adult and understand what I used not to understand' (cf. 1 Cor. 13:11).

If as a child I thought of God as distant and terrible, as an adult I have learnt to feel him nearer.

Emmanuel making the journey with us.

If in earlier days the law held sway in me, now love holds sway.

If formerly I believed in a God of martyrs, in these latter days I prefer a God who lets himself be martyred and who is friend to all human beings.

Before I set out from Egypt, the Messiah came to me, offering me weapons for the fray and inviting me to rout the foe by force; after the exodus he came to me as the Suffering Lord and Prince of Peace.

The bloody struggle against God's enemies, deep echoes of which resound through the Old Testament, was no more than a metaphor for a struggle entailing not violence but love.

It was the sign and symbol of a will set on victory where the foes are no longer Philistines or Amorites but my own besetting vices.

But there's more to it than this: that same Church which at the Second Vatican Council felt the need to rethink itself and reconsider its past in response to the challenge of the gospel, has discovered in the exodus a paradigm of its own long pilgrimage and the ancient, yet ever new, landmarks for its untiring journey to eternal life.

As the people of God, how gladly we retrace the stages of an ever newer, ever more adult reality.

As I see it, the Church is all exodus now, a great becoming of things which have always been there but which, thanks to new light from God, are now becoming clearer, in some cases even because of our own frailty and immaturity.

How can we grasp the concept of our becoming, if not in terms of this age-old patient march?

Without feeling the need to immerse ourselves in the lived experience of the people of God, compounded of sorrows and sins yet above all sustained by hope?

Culture, theology, morality all have their part in our exodus, just as they all contribute to the growing child, to the youngster developing into an adult, to the sinner who repents.

We are not born as brothers and sisters: we become them.

We aren't born chaste: we can become so.

We aren't born perfect: we try to be.

And all in the toil, stress, time, experience of living.

What doesn't Exodus teach us!

And lastly, it has taught me to be patient with the Church.

Initially, the Church seemed intolerable to me with its compromises and shortcomings.

Once I grasped that the compromises and shortcomings were my own, that the sins thickly accumulating were mine, I began to feel the same compassion for the Church that I already felt for all those travelling with me through the desert.

Exodus taught me not to judge so hastily, to see the sinfulness in my own displays of complacency, to realise that I was a hypocrite, yes, a hypocrite, as Jesus rightly says.

I insist: the true maturing of the individual takes place in exodus and in this continuous becoming lies the root of individual perfection.

I repeat it: we aren't born as brothers to our brothers, as sisters to our sisters.

By nature we are, as Genesis makes plain, hostile to one another, quarrelsome and prepared to sell our brother into slavery.

But, having suffered, having seen the tears run down the aged, wrinkled face of our father Jacob, we can say as Judah said to Pharaoh: 'I'm the one who ought to pay; if you want a hostage, take me and let beloved Benjamin go back to his father' (cf. Gen. 44:33f).

What a long time it took to explain even to Abraham, who was a man who took life seriously, that he would do better to compose his differences with his cousin Lot than to have him as an enemy!

Which one of us can observe a single one of God's commandments without the schooling of the exodus?

And here I intend to be very simple and direct, in order to help anyone who may need it.

I give one example, though a weighty one.

Before the Council, we witnessed the torments of a Church trying desperately to resolve the deep-seated problems of matrimonial morality.

We all remember the anguish colouring the pontifical documents of Pius XII, even more so those of Paul VI.

In reaction to the breakdown caused by unrestrained immorality, there was a smell of panic in the air, as though the battle were lost beyond recall.

Humanae Vitae was no small proof of this.

These pontifical documents seemed to me to be designed as a sort of trap, to spring up and catch the wolf by the paw when he was already inside the Church's sheepfold.

It puzzled me.

And yet?

Can a pope, can I, say what conflicts with things already said with so much toil and sweat?

Can you imagine a pontiff saying things contradicting his predecessors?

That contraception is permitted, that it's OK to take the pill and things like that?

Impossible.

Truth is truth and we know there's nothing more to be said, except in its defence. Cost what that may.

It's unthinkable and no one supposes otherwise.

So where's the error?

Where's the mistake in a trap designed to snap shut in the path of some poor wretch who can't grasp the import of certain truths for which he hasn't been prepared?

But who wants to lead a Christian life.

The error – and you must forgive a poor man, a truly poor man of the desert, for telling you this . . .

The error lies in the tone.

Lies in announcing a solemn principle, a terrible principle, in a bellow to break the immature silence of a pagan age unable to grasp the truth.

Brothers and sisters, even morality needs to go through its exodus, needs patience, needs much love.

The same patience, all said and done, as God has had and has with us when we don't succeed in grasping what he wants.

Which of us can live a single one of the commandments without the schooling of the exodus?

Be it the sixth commandment or the first: it's just the same.

God calls us to perfection because he is perfect; he invites us to be holy because he is holy; but he has to allow us plenty of time since gestation is long and the task by no means simple.

I only wish those who don't believe me and doubt the truth of this would pause for a moment over the first of the two commandments in which Jesus summed up the whole law.

And the first, Jesus says, is the most important one.

It isn't anything trivial.

Do you believe yourselves able, at the outset of your spiritual life, to live this first commitment which God has thought needful to ask of us and which, for our part, we feel exactly corresponds to our own deepest aspirations?

You must love the Lord your God with all your heart, with all your soul, and with all your mind. (Matt. 22:37)

Answer up!

Can you do it?

And can you live the second commandment, which is similar and says:

You must love your neighbour as yourself (Matt. 22:39)?

Which of us loves our neighbour as well as we love ourself?

And if you are dubious how to answer – for you'll need all Deuteronomy and the prophets at least to get you even half-way there – why be so harsh with unfortunate married couples who, surrounded and weakened as they are by a dominant pagan culture, feel more and more alienated from you as a result; while you, sure only in your principles, can't patiently, lovingly, tactfully bridge the gap between yourselves and their troubled consciences?

I'm not saying that you are wrong; what I am saying is, your terms are unsuitable if they are not based on a pastoral theory which takes into account the course married people ought to take and will take, if you help them and don't slap their faces during the first lesson.

The covenant, and all that it implies, between Yahweh and Israel, even more so the gospel and the Beatitudes which are its synthesis, are goals to which we have to advance by trial and error.

I try to love my God.

I try to be chaste because he lives in me.

I try to be poor, to be able to run faster to the kingdom.

How can you make such difficult demands without allowing time?

Without letting people mature?

Without sharing the march?

Many a time I've found myself facing hundreds of engaged couples and having to address them in the name of the Church, in the name of our pastors, on birth-control and contraception.

What good would it do to begin with the famous principles?

Discouragement, pessimism.

And the result?

Years later, those hundreds of couples whom I had catechised would still be at square one and, what's more, for sure with no children.

What does this mean?

It means they need time, and well I know it.

So I am not discouraged.

God knows.

God can do it.

God will help me.

But meanwhile I start from small beginnings.

I start by talking about the journey, about the sustained struggle to be waged against personal self-centredness, about the need and beauty of being fruitful, about the joy of living by the gospel.

And things will change, but only a little at a time, as Exodus shows: where a desert that could be crossed on a decent camel in fifteen days engaged the people's efforts for forty years.

Let's take another example.

That of the just or unjust war, of violence or non-violence.

People don't talk about anything today except liberation theology: whether to condemn it or applaud it.

What are we to say?

Are Cardinal Ratzinger and the Roman Curia right to be dubious about it, or are the Christians of Latin America right when they defend it?

But we can also ask ourselves: was St Thomas right in speaking about the just war and the right of the oppressed to overthrow tyranny by force; or was St Francis right in approaching the wolf without a bill-hook, armed only with love and non-violence?

The answer is simple: it depends on the degree of maturity we've reached in the course of our exodus.

Moses would have laughed at St Francis and his non-violence.

But a modern Christian doesn't laugh; in Francis's action he senses the strength of love and the superiority of non-violence over violence.

What we can therefore truly say is that a prophecy exists but not everyone is able to accept it.

There are those who are mature enough for the prophecy or for the Beatitudes, and there are those who are not.

How can I condemn the poor Christians of Latin America, in countries where a few families hold all the power and own all the land?

How can I condemn them if, subjected to such evident injustice, they form militant trade unions which the government refuses to recognise, or join insurrectionary movements?

I can remind them that non-violence is superior, that the way of love is superior and indeed more efficacious in achieving justice and building a peaceful society.

But I can't impose it on them.

The Beatitudes can't be imposed.

And that is why, when faced with these intellectual crises, these complex moral problems, we ought at least to make clear to everyone that there's a political level and there's a prophetic level.

It's hard to turn politics into prophecy where peoples still preoccupied with the logic of domination, brute force and money are concerned.

All too often we forget to make it clear that murmuring in the desert is one thing and living the Beatitudes maturely with Christ is another.

All too often the Church omits to make this distinction, not taking account of the fact that the word of God, so clearly proclaimed in Exodus, has to be obeyed in the conditions of everyday life.

All life is an exodus: hence the occasional need to respect diverse positions determined by differing factors – signs of the times, as Pope John would have said, which aren't always easy to interpret.

I mustn't forget one further thing, perhaps the most important Exodus experience of all.

There is a sea to be crossed and this sea God alone can divide for me, weak as I am, and, I may say, only at the moment I've reached maturity.

5
The Desert

The second stage of the journey is the desert.

The desert is no geographical expression but a spiritual reality.

Desert means quest for silence, peace, austerity, solitude.

Desert means intimacy, true, strong intimacy with the divine.

'Remember, Israel? Remember when I took you with me into the desert?' (cf. Hosea).

'I wanted to see what was in your heart; I wanted to confront you with the idols you were carrying with you tied to your camel-saddle and hiding from me' (cf. Gen. 31:34).

The desert will help you, purify you, make you truer, more real, freer.

Come with me.

Yesterday I called it purgatory but that was an ugly-sounding name.

Today, call it intimacy, like me.

Yesterday you looked on it as punishment, now you see it as reward; for it is a reward to spend days alone with your God.

If the exodus symbolises our journey towards perfection, the desert is where the journey has to take place.

In the desert we learn to know ourselves, to make our choices, as Deuteronomy says:

'I put two courses before you:
good or evil . . . Choose!' (cf. Deut. 30:15,19)

In the desert we learn the art of sustained life-giving prayer, we get used to the hardships of the journey, we come to know our own limitations, our self-centredness, our laziness, our gluttonousness and, more important still, the hidden things.

'I led you into the desert
to find out what was in your heart.' (cf. Exodus)

But more than that.

The desert is the school of intimacy with the divine, the silent boundless space in which we encounter the Absolute of God.

In the desert, the law becomes love and we discover God as a person.

It was precisely in the desert that the prophets helped the people of God discover this maturer dimension in their relationship with Yahweh: a relationship growing into friendship, covenant, dialogue, awareness, life.

And in particular Hosea, who tells how this encounter matures into conjugal love, seeing in wedlock the epitome of God's self-giving to us and in adultery the true nature of sin.

Now just listen to this:

Come, my people, come,
come with me into the desert
and there I shall speak
heart to heart with you of love.

Hosea finds no relationship more apt for explaining things than that of married life with its dramas and passion.

Do you want me to go on calling you my wife,
now you no longer regard me as your husband?
Do you want me to strip you naked
as you were when you were born?
Do you want me to turn you back to desert,
arid land without water?
Israel, O Israel!

The Lord could hardly have expressed himself more force-
fully, more vividly, more effectively in unmasking human
treachery, in laying the human heart bare and denouncing its
inner wickedness.

Every day in your heart you say
you have your expensive lovers.
Every day you think to yourself
they will give you things to wear.
Every day in your heart you believe
they will give you food to eat.
Israel, O Israel!
Why won't you grasp the fact
that I'm the one who cares for you?

It's a terrible denunciation.
Humanity, you've betrayed me.
You've always betrayed me.
Look, Israel, there isn't a tree on this hill under which you
haven't lain down to prostitute yourself. And what makes
me suffer all the more is that 'you can't grasp that I'm the
one who cares for you'.
I ought to punish you, human race; I ought to chastise
you, Israel; but I am God, not a human being, and I want
to rebuild our intimacy, I want you to come back to me.
And this is how it ends:

Trustfully let yourself be guided
by your father as he takes your hand.
Try once more to grasp that I
am the one who cares for you.
And be sure that I shall always love you,
Israel, O Israel!

The hope that we shall return dominates God's mind; the
certainty that the wife will understand, repent, turn back,
inspires his song:

Behold, the day is coming
when I shall renew my covenant with you.
Behold, the day is dawning
when I shall marry you again.
Behold, the day is here
when I shall reveal myself to you once more,
Israel, O Israel!

(Biblical Song by Pierangelo Comi)

The prophets regarded the relationship between husband and wife as the finest metaphor for expressing the love between God and the human race.

Jesus was to express it through the relationship between father and son. But both these relationships require solitude if they are to be analysed and plumbed to their depths.

Hosea did it in the desert sands of the exodus.

Jesus, in the desert of Gethsemane under the olive trees:

Father, for you everything is possible.
Take this cup away from me.
But let it be as you, not I, would have it. (Mark 14:36)

The divine-human relationship is essentially one of solitude.

Prayer, true crucified prayer will lead you there and there burst into a flame of love.

I suppose the longer part of our solitude with God will not take place on earth.

Down here we have too much to distract us, too many other things to think about.

Most human beings die before savouring that solitude.

Death takes them unawares with their heads full of plans and their hearts cluttered up with futile loves.

But then comes the transition, nearly always a surprise for everyone, as Jesus says in the gospel, but none the less as serious as certain.

And the transition takes us precisely where we've always tried not to go, to the very place we always avoided, busying ourselves with matters we considered more interesting and useful.

But they weren't.

Yes, the 'transition', or death as we commonly call it, takes us into a new reality, into a new dimension.

A reality and dimension still linked to earth but rather different.

The true desert.

In the old days this was called purgatory, but it's the same thing.

It's a place, an ionosphere Teilhard de Chardin called it, where there is perfect silence, perfect peace and where 'reminiscence' will be our new mode of life, just as steam is 'reminiscence' of water, the same thing albeit in a different form.

In this dimension we shall have all the time we need for prayer, meditation, contemplation.

But above all we shall have time to weep for our sins, almost all of them being sins of omission.

Yes, we shall repent for what we have not done, for the love we didn't give, for the patience we lacked, for the intimacy we neglected, for the charity we failed to practise.

Just so.

Purgatory or the desert, whatever you please to call it, is the place where the journey is completed, where we do things properly we didn't do properly on earth, whether owing to immaturity, malice or thoughtlessness.

There, will be all the time we need, no clocks there, no time-wasting visits.

Those who've made the transition in their mother's womb, the unborn, for instance, will have to make the entire journey there; those who've covered a stage or two here on earth will complete their journey there undisturbed.

The infinite will stretch before us and the pillar of fire won't be lacking to guide our steps.

Darkness will be the order of the day, made bearable by faith, hope and charity such as we have known on earth and shall need no less.

There will of course be the freedom to turn back, but no

one will have any interest in reversing course, since behind
it will be too hot, given the proximity of hell, which will be
there if only to scare the sillier and more inquisitive ones
among us.

In fact, though, I'm sure we shall keep on marching
forward, towards the land from now on truly promised and
quite near.

The stages will have to be taken in order, without rushing
them.

I mean, of freeing ourselves from idols if we haven't
already done so on earth, of crossing the Red Sea once and
for all, of consenting to be purged of deceit and self-
centredness, of learning the catechism of salvation, of getting
accustomed to trusting in our guide, the Absolute of God,
of attacking Jericho if we haven't already attacked it on earth.
And, above all, we have to get to know Jesus our elder
brother, our unique exemplar and our all.

And it will be Jesus himself who teaches us and leads us
into the final, decisive stage, that of the cross.

He will teach us what it is to die of love.

If on earth we died of indigestion, now we shall have to
die of love.

If on earth we suffered at the hands of those who hated
us, here we shall have to die for our enemies in order to save
them.

This will be quite clear to anyone who understands and
lives by the gospel.

Don't you agree?

That leaves the matter of the complaints we made at every
stage throughout the desert journey.

'Why couldn't you have let us stay in Egypt where there
was food to eat and plenty of it?'

When the meat ran out and we ate manna, we complained:
'The cooking pots were full of meat in Egypt, and now
you've led us here to eat this tasteless stuff' (cf. Exod. 16–17).

Throughout the journey we've complained.

We've filled the desert with our complaining.

But we shan't get out of the desert if we don't change our complaints into Beatitudes first.

We have to get as far as saying:

Blessed are the hungry.

Blessed are the thirsty.

Blessed . . . blessed . . . blessed!

The desert truly is the place of God and the place where we learn to become God.

Children of God, I mean, but of the same nature as God.

Whoever achieves the transformation is charity, and once charity reigns there will be no more need for faith or hope, since they will have served their purpose.

The desert, then, is the human march towards the Promised Land, the place where the Absolute of God is manifest and where we learn to be with him, talk to him, pray with him and know the compassion of the Father's heart, whose real nature is love, love alone, all love.

We leave the desert certain that God journeys with us, loves, saves and seeks us; that for us he is the All and that there is no other God but him.

6

The Dark Night

Sooner or later during the desert journey we have to experience the dark night.

Gradually the journey leads us to a point where human resources fail us and we are forced to halt in terror.

In the dark night we have only the stars to steer by, by a reality, that is to say, no longer of this world.

And this is when we begin to realise how far we are surpassed by the divine and how different God's thoughts are from our thoughts.

A hard but necessary lesson if we are to penetrate the mystery.

All the while you trust to your own reason, you cannot know God.

God is the unknowable one, and the cloud enfolding him is called the Cloud of Divine Unknowing.

We have to consent to enter that cloud before we can go beyond.

Beyond is the pure transcendence of God, the mystery of the Absolute, the root of that which is denied to human pride.

In this dark night we learn to know the things that really count.

The love of God and the reason for things.

And these are only known by revelation.

On this night
Christ burst the bonds of death

61

and rose triumphant and glorious
from the grave.

These are words based on the *Exultet*, the hymn the
Church sings deep in the night of divine unknowing.
How can we grasp?
How believe that death can be conquered?
How imagine the possibility of the resurrection?
More than that: how believe that the innocent have to pay?
How accept the apparent victory of evil over good?
How conceive that life can come through non-life, and
holiness from guilt?
For a moment we have to be ready to understand nothing
any more and put our faith in the improbable.
And yet, as though sent mad by such deep darkness, the
Church cries out:

O happy fault!
O happy fault!
O happy fault!
O happy fault!

I don't understand but I accept.
I accept the improbable: that sin, that guilt can be
overcome.
And the hymn goes on, in the confidence required of us:

How wonderful the condescension
of your love towards us, Lord.
How far beyond all reckoning
your loving-kindness, Lord.
To ransom the slave,
you consigned your Son to death,
your only Son, Jesus.

The desert has led me into this dark night.
And I can't get out of it again except through the madness
of love.
Meanwhile here I am in this dark night,

'where a pillar of light
dissipates the darkness of evil,
washes sins away,
restores innocence to the fallen,
humbles the mighty,
reconciles souls,'
doing my best to understand.
How can I?
Is there no alternative to suffering for us?
Must we really pass through it? Didn't Christ agonising in Gethsemane also think there might be some alternative?

Is it really necessary, Father, for me to die, for evil to triumph as before?

Is there no other possible solution?

Will the human race, seeing me crucified, find it any easier to believe in your love?

Will they be convinced that you care for them and are concerned for their welfare?

Wouldn't it be better, Father, to solve the world's problems?

We could do it! You are God.

Why not give everyone a house?

Why not give food, happiness, freedom to your people?

Is it really necessary to pass through death?

Do we have to lose?

Do we have to demoralise your little ones by our defeat?

Will they understand?

Is there no alternative, Father, to this night?

No.

No, none. None that doesn't admit the explosiveness of the divine.

The solutions we should like for the problems would still be based on human calculation, would only be limited solutions, earth-bound, destined for death.

God goes further.

He goes where no one has been before, into the infinite.

The new revelation will astonish many.

'Before it, the mighty will cover their faces
and kings will bow their heads.'

In the dark night, God intends to conquer as no one has
ever conquered before.
The revelation of the Suffering Servant will have conquered
our doubts for ever.
His alone the victory, his the victory!

O night of purest joy
alone accounted worthy to know the day
and the hour of Christ's resurrection from the dead!
This is the night of which the Scripture says:
the night shall be as bright as day
and the night shall light up my joy.

(*Exultet*)

Such the explosiveness of the divine solutions.
Such the improbable that becomes reality and becomes
salvation.
How can you go on doubting after hearing this?
Why don't you roll about with joy at knowing this?
Many a time I've gone into ecstasy on hearing this song
of salvation.
God has saved me.
He has saved me, a slave, a sinner; he has opened heaven
for me, has descended on my path, has come into my tent.
No more uncertainty. He has said it: now we travel
forward, hand in hand.
Now salvation has come, heaven is earth, and earth heaven.

Do not remember the things that are past.
Do not think of the old things any more.
Look, I'm making something new.
It's actually sprouting – surely you can see it?
Listen, says the Lord, he who has made a path through
the sea:

Don't be afraid, I am with you.
Don't be afraid, I have ransomed you.
I'm selling Egypt to ransom you.
For you, I'm bartering nations.
Don't be afraid.
I am with you.
Don't be afraid
of anywhere
where I shall draw you to me.

(Biblical Song by Pierangelo Comi)

The dark night teaches me to believe, since merely to understand is a trivial thing, unworthy of love. Understanding is a human thing; believing is divine.

When I understand I lay hold on earth; when I believe I lay hold on heaven.

When I understand, I meditate; when I believe, I contemplate.

When I understand, I am here; when I believe, I am there, beyond.

Such is the very nature of things that have to be overcome by faith.

The activity of a soul bound up in God is contemplation.

The cloud of unknowing that separated me from my God now unites me to him, binds me to him and forces me to ask:

What was my meditation?
Mere doubt.
What is contemplation now?
Certainty.
Before, I travelled at my own pace.
Now, I travel at God's pace.
Before, I was here.
Now, I am beyond.
Before, I used to touch the visible.
Now, I am enfolded in the invisible.
Before, I used to talk; now, I pray.

And, in ecstasy, I sing:

O blissful night
in which the Egyptians were despoiled
and the Hebrews enriched.
Night in which heaven
is reconciled to earth,
God is united to the human race
and becomes one with us.

(cf. Exultet)

You in me and I in you.
What more can you have?

The dark night has death itself as the final ordeal.

When by faith I discovered that physical death is only a sign and can alter nothing since I am eternal, I then began wondering what the function of this sign could be, since it is regarded as being so important and fills so many people with dread.

What is this sign intended to show us, carrying us off in our tenth, our twentieth, our seventieth year?

To be logical meanwhile, we ought to call it crossing, transition, passover, since we are talking about a true transition, a genuine crossing, a real passover, such as we call the death-and-resurrection of Jesus.

And, in all faith, we are convinced of this: it is no more than a transition, it is no more than a crossing.

It's like a door, with a 'this side' and a 'that side'.

This side is earthly experience, that side is the space beyond earth – purgatory, desert, reminiscence, call it what you please – to which my personality passes over.

But everything still goes on, since we are animated by the eternal life bestowed on us by God at the moment of conception.

If, then, we insist on calling this 'death', as the Word himself often called it, we ought to attach its proper meaning to it: its true liturgical meaning.

When Pope John felt he was approaching the transition, death, and heard the crowds praying for him in St Peter's Square, he said:

'This is my bed, this is the altar. Let us go up, celebrate the mass and complete the sacrifice.'

So doing, Pope John gave death its true significance: a liturgy. In dying, we celebrate our maturest mass.

The bowing of the head of the living, the fading of the flower, the end of a stage, the coming of evening, the slaughter of an animal, the death of a human being, are all aspects of a solemn mass celebrated by the universe before its Creator. It is lovingly saying to the maker and sustainer of all things who guides all things towards perfection: 'Here I am. Take me as I am. You are the All and I give you all.'

I truly believe the moment of death, especially if we are mature and conscious, is the mass we each of us celebrate on the world as priests of the eternal.

It is the 'yes' of creation to its Creator, the amen of believers enabled through Christ to make a priestly offering to their God as Absolute, as Alpha and Omega, as the One.

'Thy will be done' is the phrase that sums up the true quality of this offering, as the will of God's creature melts into the sweet will of God, accepted through and through.

Love yearns no more and the child rejoins the Father, fulfilling its entire existence in a total act of love.

There's a song used by Neo-Catechumenal Way communities called *Akedà!*

Based on a Hebrew hymn, it puts the following fine words about sacrifice into the mouth of Isaac.

This is how it goes:

It was still dark
when Abraham got ready
to sacrifice his son.
They looked each other in the eye,
then Isaac said:
Akedà, akedà, akedà, akedà,
Bind me, bind me tightly, Father,
so that I can't resist,
or the sacrifice will be worthless
and both of us be rejected!

There on the mountain-top I see the altar of stones they have built together; the son has understood his father's will; humbly, generously, he gets ready to be sacrificed.

As creature, he is afraid; as son, he wishes to do his father's will.

And he asks to be bound, tightly bound, so that he won't flinch when the knife goes in.

What binds is faith, and by it we overcome our weakness when love summons us.

The song goes on:

Come and see faith on earth,
the father sacrificing his only son
and the beloved son offering his throat.

(Song by Chico Arguello)

This prefigures the mass to be celebrated on Calvary and, later still, on every altar.

The mass we each and every Isaac have to say: the mass of the Father sacrificing Jesus his Son.

This is love lived to the extreme.

The total gift of self.

After living a mass like that, what else can there be for us but love's eternal kingdom?

All darkness in this life is a preparation for that mass.

All sorrow schools us for that mass.

All aridity in prayer is an anticipation of that mass.

Every death is a living of that mass.

Jesus lived it to the very depths, and the depths were the mouth of the fish that swallowed Jonah for three whole days.

In the case of Jesus, the living One, the mass thus celebrated on Calvary was the most authentic testimony he could offer to the content of his message of love, and the Church has made it her own by putting it at the centre of the Easter liturgy.

But this pattern, this dying of love, was already written into the whole creation. It is the theme of the entire universe.

The dawns and sunsets of earth, birth and death, the light

of the stars and the collapse of worlds, joy and sorrow, the
rise of states and the decline of peoples, all manifest that
same reality.

Teilhard de Chardin was to write his finest pages in his
Mass on the World, a liturgy indeed for elect spirits,
researchers and scientists, and all who perceive the essential
unity between science and faith, the visible and the invisible,
heaven and earth, God and the human race.

7

The Kingdom

However dark the night may be and however hard-going be faith, they cannot conceal the kingdom from me.

For the kingdom to be visible is essential to me in my weakness.

What would become of us if there were no kingdom?

Everything is governed by this hope and from it I draw the energy for my journey.

Gradually the kingdom reveals itself to me, not so much as an institution or anything of that sort, but as a person summoning me, trying to establish a more and more intimate, friendly, living relationship with me.

The kingdom is the home of the King: his divine essense of peace, justice, mercy and truth.

This essence fascinates and surrounds me, it seeks me out and conquers me.

I started with my exodus, I've now crossed the desert and endured the dark night.

Before me lies the kingdom, within my reach at last.

There it is, object of all my hope.

On their desert journey the Hebrews had the Promised Land for goal. We have the kingdom for our goal, the Promised Land being a figure and prophecy of it.

The Promised Land was an objective appropriate to people needing a country where they could enjoy their freedom.

The kingdom responds to the need we all have, to see, to hear, to serve the King who is God himself.

As we gradually mature in the things of the spirit, earth

fades into a sign and we set out in search of what it used to represent: the very person of God.

Reality, all reality is a person.

The law is a person, heaven is a person, God is person, just as we are persons.

The relationship between persons is different from that existing between things. It summons us to harmony, dependence, love, humility, service, dedication, the offering of one to the other.

In a word, it's an intimate relationship of shared plans, tireless, lively exchange, mutual, happy achievement.

We shall never get tired of contemplating the kingdom, of the joy of having reached it, and possessing it, of living its essence with the King.

Hence all our sadness and fears are baseless.

From the moment the kingdom becomes our heritage and destiny, joy alone can hold sway in our lives.

The kingdom is the answer to all desires, the justification of all expectation and the fulfilment of everything achieved.

It is satisfaction.

So we mustn't be astonished if it takes us much sweat and long travelling before we can possess it.

We mustn't be surprised if we need to be purified before setting foot on its soil.

Great the demands of the kingdom, and conquering it demands total commitment.

Indeed, in the gospel the kingdom is likened to a treasure hidden in a field, to a precious pearl, bought with all one possesses.

It is likened to ten virgins ordered to keep watch by night for the coming of the bridegroom; also, to a net cast into the sea, bringing up good fish and bad and bringing them ashore to be sorted out.

The severity of the kingdom, as portrayed by Matthew, is no less than the terrible judgment exacted on us at our life's end by the law of love:

I was hungry
and you never gave me food,

I was thirsty
and you never gave me anything to drink,
I was naked
and you never gave me clothes. (Matt. 25:42f)

The kingdom goes on developing even when you're not
paying attention or when you're asleep (cf. Matt. 4:26–9). It
can transform the tiniest things into things large enough to
shelter the fowls of the air (cf. Matt. 4:30–2).

The kingdom is the arrival-point of the journey beginning
that far-away day when you were conceived in your mother's
womb.
    And this is why your conception was such an important
event: it was programmed within the planning of the
kingdom.
    God is the beginning and the end, the Alpha and Omega.
    He was the programmer, he will produce the result, he
who is the living One.
    We are eternal since, given our beginning from the act of
love, we shall, sustained by the living One, reach a blessed
eternity.
    Though our journey has involved a long delay, now we
possess.
    No one can ever take this possession away from us.
    We have endured the loneliness; now we possess the power
of total communication.
    We were orphans?
    Now we have a Father.
    We were only children?
    Now we have brothers and sisters.
    We had no friends?
    Now we have a Friend.
    We were sterile?
    Now we are fruitful.
    We were inadequate?
    See, the victory of freedom.

But above all, were we lonely? Behold the bridegroom.

And this is best of all, for him we were seeking.

The kingdom yearns for the King and the King yearns for the Queen.

Listen prayerfully to this exaltation of the highest of all loving relationships, the grand harmony of the universe, the reality at the heart of the kingdom.

This is what it says in Psalm 45:

My heart is stirred by a noble theme,
I address my poem to the King,
    my tongue the pen of an expert scribe.
Of all men you are the most handsome,
gracefulness is a dew on your lips,
    for God has blessed you for ever.
Warrior, strap your sword to your side,
in your majesty and splendour advance, ride on
in the cause of truth, gentleness and justice.
Stretch tight the bowstring,
    lending terror to your right hand . . .
Your throne will endure for ever,
    the sceptre of your Kingdom a sceptre of justice;
    you love uprightness and detest evil.
This is why God, your God, has anointed you
with oil of gladness, as none of your rivals.

And then, turning to the Queen:

Listen, my daughter, attend to my words and hear:
forget your own nation and your ancestral home,
then the King will fall in love with your beauty.
He is your Lord, bow down before him.
From Tyre they will court your favour with gifts,
the richest of peoples with jewels set in gold.
Clothed in brocade, the king's daughter is led within
to the King with the maidens in her retinue;
her companions are brought to her,
they enter the King's palace with joy and rejoicing.
Instead of your ancestors you will have sons;
you will make them rulers over the whole world.

I shall make your name endure from generation to
    generation,
so nations will sing your praise for ever and ever.

Last night I felt like reading the Book of Esther again. It's a
short book but a very attractive one.

I find it particularly so now, since, talking of the King and
his kingdom, in Esther I glimpse the function and role of the
Queen.

May the Lord forgive me and not impute what I have done
to pride.

In my spiritual life I have always been so confounded by
the thought of my own poverty and abjection as to have
developed a complex. The nothingness-complex: that, being
nothing, I was no good at any type of prayer.

Brothers and sisters, did you know, I've never really
mastered intercessory prayer?

Did you know, when people ask me to pray for them, I
immediately think my prayers won't have any effect?

What can I do?

What effect can I have on the King's heart? On God's
heart?

Yes, I admit it: thanks to a false humility, I've never got
the hang of intercessory prayer.

At least, so it seemed to me yesterday evening.

And then I read, there once was a king called Ahasuerus.

And I read that a wretch called Haman was trying to dupe
him into slaughtering all the people of God.

The lovely Esther, a daughter of this people, was Queen
at the court of Ahasuerus.

She got to hear of the king's plan and resolved to help her
people, even at cost of her life.

Prayer was Esther's only recourse and this was how she
prayed:

'My God, my King, the Only One,
come to my help for I am alone
and have no helper but you.
Remember, Lord,

reveal yourself in the time of our distress
and give me courage . . .
You see the affliction of your people.
Save us by your hand
and come to our help,
for we have no one but you.' (cf. Est. 4)

That was how Esther interposed between king and people.
And King Ahasuerus, thanks to Esther's intercession,
decided not to liquidate the Hebrew nation.

For me last night, Esther, the favourite wife, the Queen
near and dear to the king's heart, became my summons to
intercessory prayer, the type of prayer which I had been no
good at, owing to the faint-hearted way I made my petitions.
Due to a funny kind of false humility, I didn't have the
guts to ask.
I didn't see myself as a Queen in the presence of the King.
I saw myself as a worm, and this prevented me from grasping
that humility is truth; and that the truth is, God loves me as
I am.
I am a worm, it's true, but it's also true God loves me as
a Queen in spite of my being a worm.
In fact, listen to what the Word says as the final revelation.
We are at the last book in the Bible: the Apocalypse.
For an ecstatic moment let us see things through the eyes
of John, Jesus's best friend.
John sees clearly, since his eyes are full of love for his
God.
And what does he see?
He sees us having reached the end of the journey, sees us
as a bride about to meet her bridegroom, as a Queen about
to meet the King.
The kingdom is there, the gates fly open, the everlasting
doors stand wide.
Enter the King of glory.
What about us?
Where's the one I programmed by an act of love down in
earthly exile, summoned to freedom from slavery, purified

from idols? Where's the one I taught the darkness of God's
absence, gave the courage to believe and the strength to hope,
gave victory over inadequacy as a foretaste of God's gifts and
infused with free, crucified love?
Step forward, and see what you mean to me!

'Come here and I shall show you
the bride that the Lamb has married.'
In the spirit, the Angel carried me
to the top of a very high mountain
and showed me the holy city, Jerusalem,
coming down from heaven, from God,
dressed as a bride for her bridegroom,
glittering like some precious jewel,
like a crystal-clear diamond.
I could not see any temple in it
since the Lord God Almighty and the Lamb
were themselves the temple,
and the city did not need
the sun or the moon for light,
since it was lit by the glory of God
and its lamp was the Lamb.
The curse of destruction will be abolished.
The throne of God and the Lamb
will be in the city . . .
And night will be abolished.
They will not need lamplight or sunlight,
because the Lord God will be shining on them.
And they will reign for ever and ever.
(Rev. 21:9–11,22–3; 22:3–5)

Are you still afraid after that?
My little aborted Israel, are you still afraid?
And now repeat with me, over and over:
'Come, Lord Jesus!' (Rev. 22:20).

8

'In God Alone Is Rest for My Soul'*

We may not perhaps quite realise what trusting to God on the human journey means.

This trust is in fact the most radical leap of all.

The Psalm says:

'Whoever trusts in the Lord is like Mount Zion, unshakeable, firm-set for ever' (Ps. 125:1).

And that's true, absolutely true.

Trust casts out fear, makes faith easier, gives a thrust to hope.

Trust in God helps you to feel near him, to see him as the solution to all problems, even the most abstruse.

Trust is the greatest joy in our relationship with God.

Whoever trusts in God has already covered the hardest part of the journey.

He is now in sight of Jericho; victory is at hand.

A victory filled with delight and boundless love.

God, you are my God, I can count on you.

When the representatives of five continents met in Mexico City a few years ago to discuss birth control in the context of the serious problem of world hunger, the questions they asked were:

What to do?

How to do it?

The information exchanged between these representatives of five continents wasn't calculated to buttress the already badly shaken confidence of anyone frightened of dying of hunger because of the rapidly increasing number of mouths to be fed.

And if things go on like this, in the next century . . .

What can one reply?

To anyone knowing nothing of prophecy, there isn't much room for discussion and the conclusion is simple:

We must limit births.

We must distribute contraceptives.

If need be, we must sterilise – women first, since they're more easily led, and then the men.

And a modern, radical, pagan culture will be the result: a culture for our times, in which no one will have any worries and which will gradually conquer the world with its apparently realistic approach and its certainty of having got things right.

What else can you do?

Formerly staunch opponents of innovation, the Chinese have already coined the slogan: 'Two-child family, perfect family; three children, big crowd.'

The Indians, more particularly Indian women, are badgered with indiscreet visits until shamed into accepting sterilisation.

In every case the simple, the defenceless, the poor are the ones on whom the onus falls.

Christians are all too often content with making protests, proposing natural methods and recommending their own humanitarian devices.

We can safely say, the prophetic dimension is completely lacking.

The same thing happens over armaments.

People say, 'Don't be childish. Look at it seriously. How can you put up a case for unilateral disarmament?

'Can you really imagine that would lead to peace?

'Politics and morality are two different things.'

It's terrible but that's the way it is.

Faith is dead and buried, true enough.

Yes, faith is buried.

When I was young and considering getting married, I used to enjoy discussing this with a friend of mine called Ernest.

He was one of the few who really shared my faith; simple as it was, it still keeps me going today.

'If I get married, I mean to regard God and God alone as the programmer of my children's births, the electronic brain uniquely able to regulate my wife's fertility cycles, to control her temperature and so forth, and in particular to give me the number of children I can cope with without my being driven into the ground.'

Ernest did in fact get married and act accordingly, bear witness accordingly, believe accordingly.

He now has seven children who haven't driven him into the ground, starved him to death or ever given him cause for regret.

I didn't get married since God hadn't programmed things thus, and so haven't been able to bear witness to my faith in this way.

Instead I'm trying to bear witness to it in the words I'm saying to you today, many years later.

Courageous Ernest used to say to me, 'I'm not the kind of man to make love by the thermometer or the calendar. I'm a child of God and should feel ashamed to upset my Father's plans in important matters affecting him so nearly, I mean, about children he intends to be born.'

Ernest honestly believed that children were 'programmed' by God himself, not one more, not one less, and that the electronic calculator of the Absolute could never get things wrong, as the Billings or Ogino methods in fact very frequently do.

I make bold to believe the same and think it my duty to say as clearly as I can that if morality is safeguarded merely by human systems it has no relation whatever to the divine from the moment faith has been bestowed by God.

Rather than live by that morality, I would prefer to be a sinner.

I would rather be free.

I would rather be ignorant. I sense that standing midway between faith and reason, between prophecy and politics, weakens me and deprives me of experiencing the finest thing in life: experience of the mystery.

Either God is God, or God doesn't exist.

And just as I believe God does exist, so I believe in his electronic calculator, I believe in his infinite programming, I believe in an order based on faith, I believe in his conscious fatherhood more than I do in my own.

So do your sums, gentlemen; they will certainly come out wrong.

You will have to close down your old people's homes, you'll be left all alone in your sterility, you'll learn the horror of growing old and, worst of all, you'll learn what real suffering is: that of having no one to care for you.

The problems raised by faith and hope are infinite in dimension.

Yet they lead us back to the simplicities of childlike reasoning.

If God exists, nothing escapes his presence, his will, his order: not a cell, not even Halley's comet.

If God doesn't exist, there isn't a system but only chaos and the irrational.

How can anyone work out how many people are going to be born in the twenty-first century?

How can anyone count the number of the stars or measure the sands of the sea with a bushel basket, Job asked? (cf. Job 38; Isa. 40:12).

Besides, I prefer to believe; I prefer to hope against all hope.

How invincible I feel when I believe! What strength I acquire from hope!

And how sorry I feel for people who have neither one nor the other!

I don't think it would be disastrous to have a culture with faith as the basis of its activities.

I have nothing to lose.

You will tell me I'm being childish. You will smirk behind your hands, like the knowing, crafty rogues you are.

We shall see who proves right in the end.

Peasant culture has by no means lost the ability to believe in these things, to trust in life, to hope in the seasons, to pray to the saints and remember to pray for the dead.

We shall see whether industrial culture can do better.

It's certainly very confident in its technology and data-banks, and certainly very ingenious.

Yet I'm unimpressed, since in my country the programmers shock me by changing programmes every other minute and affront my eyes with tomatoes being deliberately crushed by dumper-trucks.

How unpleasant modern economic methods are!

What a disaster the knowing, rationalistic man is, and how she stinks like a corpse, this lady self-programmed not to have children.

And she thinks she's the clever one!

Yes, I still believe in boys like Ernest, who used to say 'I don't make love by the calendar.'

And if anyone ventures to tell me that, in the twenty-first century, and so on, and so on, we shall all starve to death, my answer will be:

Better to die of hunger than die of loneliness.

Better to die of hunger than die of boredom.

Better to die of hunger than die of drugs.

More than all else: better to die of hunger than consent to a life devoid of mystery, devoid of the Absolute, devoid of prayer.

What would I be if I lacked my God?

An atom lost in a limitless universe and, what's worse, without a centre, without a home, without a father, without siblings, without intimacy of any sort.

An atom no longer able to say its morning prayer, like this:

O God you are my God,
I pine for you,
my heart thirsts for you,

my body longs for you,
as a land parched, dreary and waterless.

Or to go on:

Thus I have gazed on you in the sanctuary,
seeing your power and your glory.
Better your faithful love than life itself;
my lips will praise you.

And again:

Thus I will bless you all my life,
in your name lifting up my hands,
all my longings fulfilled as with fat and rich foods,
a song of joy on my lips and praise in my mouth.

What a comfort to be able to say:

On my bed when I think of you,
I muse on you in the watches of the night,
for you have always been my help;
in the shadow of your wings I rejoice,
my heart clings to you
and the strength of your right hand supports me.
(Ps. 63)

Yes, nothing supports me like the strength of your right
hand.

Above all, it supports me on my journey.
I set out such a long time ago from nothing, for I was
nothing before God programmed me and my mother
conceived me.
I came into the world through no merit of my own.
Although I couldn't think, there was someone looking
after me.
Then I began to walk on my own two feet, but where was
I to go if I didn't know the way?

God was the way.

God took me by the hand.

God showed me the road.

I was often aware he was holding my hand. Often.

I was tempted to think I was going it alone, but there were plenty of occasions when I realised it was God guiding me, that without him I came to a dead-end.

The further I went, the more delicate his touch.

You could say I was being trained to freedom, that he wanted me to learn how to go on my own.

And then I felt really frightened and searched for him, since it was horrible travelling alone and the night was dark.

Faith then taught me to travel in God's company, to make my decisions with him, to live with him as wife with husband, happy in keeping nothing from each other.

There came the time when he decided to test me, as he had tested Job.

He wanted to see for himself, and make me see, whether my staying with him, my choosing him, was dictated by mere self-interest and not by love. Whether I had chosen him because he was the stronger, richer, more rewarding.

He vanished and I realised I was alone, really alone.

Now I could do whatever I liked, even choose another God if I wished.

But there was no God but him, and what I chose without him only made me wretched, thoroughly wretched.

I implored him to return and, when he judged I had had time to grasp the point, he came back at dead of night.

The clash between love and loneliness, between light and darkness, between 'yes' and 'no', was unforgettable, radical in its effect.

I understood then that without God I couldn't live, that away from him all was chaos.

A deeper trust was born, that trust identified with hope.

Now I could believe against all hope, even to the most absurd degree.

God was my God and in him all was luminous.

Programming the exact number of children my friend Ernest could cope with without worrying about birth control or accidents?

A trifle.

Finding a job for someone unemployed who was more interested in working than in money?

Done in a trice.

Bestowing fertility on a woman who can't have but wants to have children?

A pleasure indeed.

Keeping a family united, and keeping it fed and happy despite the bungling in the world?

Very easy.

Finding an unattractive girl who thinks she's been left on the shelf a loyal and loving mate prepared to share the journey with her?

Child's play.

Presenting a bishop, not afraid to ask, with ordination candidates, the egocentricity of their families notwithstanding, and letting him get on with the business of running his diocese without further worry on that score?

No problem.

Sending a cold winter to freeze the apple and olive trees, and recall to their senses people who for years have been too lazy to harvest the olives or who squash the apples with dumper-trucks?

A routine act of celestial administration.

How sweet it is to trust in the Lord. What peace of heart to feel him present in every aspect of life.

How strong I feel when I put my trust in him.

Then I can truly say with the people of God:

Whoever trusts in the Lord
is like Mount Zion,
unshakeable,
firm-set for ever. (Ps. 125:1)

Shalom! Shalom!
Shalom! Shalom!

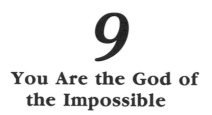

You Are the God of the Impossible

If God exists, and he does, he is the living One.

Call him Creator, call him Unmoving Mover, call him Providence, call him Absolute, call him what you please.

St Thomas called him Being.

We should think of him as he who Is, as Exodus says: 'I am he who is' (Exod. 3:14).

Charles de Foucauld loved to think of him as the God of the Impossible and I like this title too, particularly now when human knavery and refined technology threaten to deprive the poor of their sense of the divine, their sense of the mystery.

It can't be denied that, given their lack of preparation and multiple distractions, people today find it more difficult to believe in God.

A little knowledge is damaging to faith, be it said, and much knowledge alone can come to the rescue.

We are at the ford and things aren't going well for us. The two banks have receded and frequently we fear we're going to drown.

I try to save myself by studying a great deal, by praying a great deal.

Especially by praying a great deal.

It was hot that day when Abraham was sitting by the oak of Mamre.

Raising his eyes, he looked.

There were three men standing in front of him.

Hardly had he caught sight of them than he knelt on the ground and said:

'My Lord,
I beg you, don't go by without stopping.
I'll bring you a little water, and you can wash your feet
and rest in the shade.
I'll bring you a bite to eat, and you can refresh yourselves
before going any further.
Not for nothing, not by chance,
have you visited me today.' (cf. Gen. 18:1–5)

What an astounding vision this was of Abraham's at the oak of Mamre.

The three men talking, resting, refreshing themselves and gazing at Abraham as he looks happily back at them.

The eyes of the three men are the eyes of one.

It is the Lord.

The eyes of the One who long ago had asked him, the patriarch, to forsake his homeland of Ur for the land of Canaan.

'Leave your country and go' (Gen. 12:1).

And he had left it, had departed.

Now there is a closer, more intimate encounter.

'Lord, what haven't you given me? Tents, camels, carpets, sheep, wealth . . . Yet there's one thing I want much more that you haven't given me, and one day my possessions will pass to a stranger and I shall die without descendants.'

'No, Abraham . . . you will have a son. Your heritage will not pass to a stranger but to the fruit of your own loins. You will have a son.'

'And Abraham believed and this was reckoned to him as righteousness.' (cf. Gen. 15:1–6)

And Isaac was born, although this was impossible because Sarah, Abraham's wife, was sterile and he, Abraham, was a hundred years old.

God is the God of the impossible: this is the foundation-stone of faith, the grounds for our courage, our hope against all hope.

If I pray, this is why; if I believe, this is why; if I call on God, this is why.

Is there any point in praying to a God who can't do anything, can't hear, can't listen to you, can't see you?

A God of that sort is no God.

The world is full of people who believe but don't believe, of people who sit on the fence, who never resolve the problem and live in perennial doubt.

People who worship a god or more than one, who, as the psalm says satirically:

have mouths but say nothing,
have eyes but see nothing,
have ears but hear nothing,
have noses but smell nothing,
have hands but cannot feel,
have feet but cannot walk. (cf. Ps. 115:5–7)

These are gods made of silver or wood; gods that can't and never could help you.

The God of the impossible is a God who knows, a God who can, a God who provides.

He is the living One.

I'm going to tell you about an unforgettable experience I once had. Listen to this.

I was driving through a small Sahara village in my jeep.

It was hot, that day.

There was no oak of Mamre, so I took refuge in the underground passages running from house to house under the village.

The place was so hot that the villagers had dug out underground tunnels.

Inside these it was reasonably cool.

I hadn't reckoned with my ignorance of their layout and

the total darkness; so, walking along in the cool, I lost my way.

I became totally lost in the maze of underground alleys.

Getting alarmed, I started to shout and . . .

After a while a trapdoor opened above my head and a handsome Arab profile appeared against the sunlight bursting into the passage. He'd heard me shouting.

'What are you doing down there?'

'I've got lost.'

'Come on,' he said, 'get up here.'

And I climbed up some narrow steps which led into a courtyard full of light and flowers.

I remember there was a pomegranate tree shading the courtyard and a magnificent hedge of blue bougainvillea.

The Arab, who was called Bashir, forthwith unrolled a carpet and offered me some delicious tea.

We had an enthralling conversation.

Bashir lived in the village and was the organiser of a Muslim religious fraternity having its own pretty little mosque, which he took me to visit.

'I'm very lucky,' he told me. 'Allah in his generosity has given me wealth, an extended family, gardens to farm.'

Then he paused and looked at me, searching my eyes to see if he could trust me.

I told him I was a marabout, that I believed in God and had come all the way from Italy to make friends with our Muslim brothers.

'You see,' he said, 'I've one great grief. I think I may confide in you. I'm married to a good woman – a pretty one too – called Atala. Allah however hasn't blessed her with children, and this is a big problem.

'I shall have to divorce her and marry someone else.

'My relatives are very devout and look on childlessness as a grave disgrace . . . you understand?'

I looked at Bashir in silence.

He was sitting cross-legged beside me in his yellow turban.

'Bashir,' I said, 'do you believe in God?

'Do you know the story of Abraham?

'Of course you do. You Arabs solemnly celebrate Eid el-

Kebir by slaughtering a sheep to commemorate Abraham's sacrifice.

'Right, Bashir! You believe in God and I believe in God. Ask your wife Atala to join us and we will pray over her, calling on God and asking him for this gift. You'll see, Bashir. I believe . . .'

Atala came.

Bashir explained the situation to her and told her what we proposed to do.

Atala knelt down on the carpet, which had now become a little Christian-Muslim church, meekly lowered her head and I prayed as follows:

'O God of Abraham, Isaac and Jacob,
hear our prayer.
You see your servant Atala here.
Like Sarah, she has no children, she is sterile.
But you are the God of life,
the God of the impossible.
Give us a sign of your love,
hear your servant as I pray to you,
hear us, we beseech you.'

When I drove off in the jeep it was much cooler and I had to switch on my headlights before I got to Tamanrasset.

I felt happy.

Two years passed before I went through that village again, since it wasn't on my normal work-circuit.

I accelerated on catching sight of the village in the distance, and the jeep drew up in a cloud of dust even finer than the sand sent flying by the wheels.

When the cloud dispersed I saw the smiling face of Bashir, who had come out to meet me.

His eyes shone.

He ran forward with one hand in the air.

From his clenched fist protruded three fingers.

Yes, in two years, faith had presented him with three babies.

One born nine months after our prayer meeting and twins one year later.

I can't tell you what a feast we had that night under the pomegranate tree.

When it was time for me to leave, as a sign of friendship Atala opened her scent box and anointed my turban and cloak with perfumed oil.

That perfume never went away. Six months afterwards, whenever I put on my turban, I could still detect the penetrating scent Atala had sprinkled on it.

Then it was I overcame the sense of repugnance affecting the western reader of Psalm 133, where brotherly love is likened to the oil that ran off Aaron's head into his beard. It means, in fact, an expensive ointment leaving a delightful scent but no trace of grease.

Can't you believe after this?

Ever since, it has been my delight to pray with women who suppose themselves sterile. Rosary in hand, I love to repeat the words:

'God, you are my God, you are the God of the impossible.'

And faith is turned to joy.

Faith in the God of the impossible has transformed my life and driven out fear, even fear of sinning.

God is the living One.

God overcomes.

God created heaven and earth.

God led his people through the desert.

God brought them safe through the Red Sea.

God raised Jesus from the dead.

God builds his Church out of weak stones such as we are.

God gives food to the hungry.

God fills the heart with joy regardless of worldly ordeals.

God leads us into the kingdom. God can forgive us.

God loves us in spite of our sins.

God sees all.

God can do all.

God is the God of the impossible.

But the greatest thing of all is that God is my friend, my confidant, my brother, my father.
When the relationship with him is so intimate, can I have further cause for fear?
Fear that a friend will betray a friend?
Fear that a brother will forsake a brother?
Fear that a father will forget his child?
This is why Jesus told us, when you pray, pray like this: 'Our Father who art in heaven.'
He is supreme.
Inspired by that sublimity, Charles de Foucauld composed this prayer.
Listen, I invite you to say it every morning:

Father,
I abandon myself into your hands;
do with me what you will.
Whatever you may do, I thank you:
I am ready for all, I accept all.
Let only your will be done in me,
and in all your creatures.
I wish no more than this, O Lord.
Into your hands I commend my soul;
I offer it to you with all the love of my heart,
for I love you, Lord, and so need to give myself,
to surrender myself into your hands, without reserve,
and with boundless confidence,
for you are my Father.

It's hard to go further than that.

10

We Who Fought at Jericho

Humanly speaking, Jericho is an impregnable city.

On the level of mystical experience, however, it's the first ordeal we encounter on passing to 'the other side of things'.

What a staggering adventure.

We who fought at Jericho!

Our unique boast untainted by vanity.

The plenitude of spiritual experience.

We who fought at Jericho!

We saw the walls of the fortified city fall down.

We had learnt how to pray.

The divine Master's saying comes to mind: 'If your faith is the size of a mustard seed you will say to this mountain, "Move from here to there," and it will move' (Matt. 17:20).

At Jericho, the gigantic walls collapsed at the onslaught of soldiers of faith.

God willed that we could say of me, of you:

'We who fought at Jericho!'

Yes, Jericho was absolutely impregnable.

Solidly fortified, flanked by mountains from which the dressed stone had been quarried for the walls.

To the south lay a plain, a plain so flat that as far as the Dead Sea you could see any force approaching to the attack.

However, there was nothing to be done about it.

Since the Lord had given the order to attack, it had to be attacked.

If Jericho hadn't fallen, the whole Promised Land would for ever and only be a land promised but never possessed.

Now when Joshua was near Jericho,
he looked up and saw a man standing in front of him,
grasping a naked sword.
'Are you on our side or our enemies'?' he asked.
'On neither side. I have come as captain of the army of
      the Lord' . . .
'What has my Lord to say to his servant?'
The captain of the army of the Lord replied to Joshua,
'Take your sandals off your feet,
for the place where you are standing is holy.' (Jos.
5:13–15)

Joshua obeyed.
But Jericho was firmly barricaded against the Israelites: no
one came out and no one went in.
What was to be done in this impossible situation?
How do you attack a fortified city when the only weapons
you have are sticks?
Up on the walls the defenders laughed at these people,
looking as puny as an army of grasshoppers, who came
unarmed to do battle.
The Lord said to Joshua:

'Look, I am putting Jericho at your mercy.
All you warriors must march round the city praying.
Go right round the city once
and do the same on six successive days.
Seven priests must carry
seven ram's-horn trumpets in front of the ark.
On the seventh day, you will go seven times round the
      city
and the priests will blow their trumpets.
When the ram's-horn sounds,
as soon as you hear the sound of the trumpet,
the entire people must utter a mighty war cry
and the city wall will collapse then and there,
and the people will then go into the assault,
each man straight ahead.' (Jos. 6:1–5)

And the Israelites obeyed.

As the Lord had ordered, they surrounded Jericho with prayer.

They wrapped it in a cloak of faith, bound it round with the shout of hope.

Seven days later, at dawn, Joshua shouted his war cry:

'For the God of Israel!'
and flung himself against those walls so well-laid and impregnable.

And Jericho fell of its own accord: the walls collapsed and everyone could see the power of the Lord.

The significance of this battle is obvious, and God teaches his people this great lesson.

God is the God of the impossible.

To him all things are possible.

Learn this, Israel.

Make the earth quake with your prayers, not with your arms.

Faith is your victory, hope is your might.

The days are gone when things were made visible by human brawn.

The era of the invisible has begun.

'What do I care about your strength?

What I want is your love.

What do your calculations matter?

What I want is your trust.

I want you, you alone.

If you trust in me, you will conquer.'

To fight at Jericho is to experience God, an experience so great it can never be erased from our hearts.

It will stay in the memory.

Do you remember, Israel?

Daniel, do you remember?

You came to me in all your poverty.

Though crushed by the weight of your nothingness, you rose from the depths of your misery.

'How could this possibly have happened?

'A thousand times over, I've proved it.

'I was a drug-addict.

'Degradation was all the future had in store for me.

'With all my soul I dived into my nothingness, like a heavy stone plummeting to the bottom.

'They said to me: Take heart, raise the war cry and fly towards the walls with all the energy of desperation.

'"For the God of Israel!"

'I rushed forward, keeping my eyes shut so as only to see the invisible.

'When I opened them again, the walls had collapsed and I was picking my way through the debris.

'I had won.'

Brothers and sisters, you who hear my words, I want to share this experience, this unique experience with you.

Then you will be invincible and happiness will return to reign in your heart.

If you succeed in believing, victory is yours.

If you can hope, you will see the impossible become possible.

Many a time I've cried, when faced with those enslaved to drugs, alchohol or sexual obsessions: Oh, if you only knew! If you could only believe that Christ is the Saviour! If only you could not doubt!

Try spending night after night in prayer, try fasting as much as your strength will allow, try weeping until you fall into convulsions.

Then you will see!

Yes, we who fought at Jericho bear witness to a new fact.

When we heard the ram's-horn sounding with the breath of faith, we watched the inconceivable: the walls fell down.

O divine adventure of the Spirit!

O experience of the living God!

Remember, Leonard, when you came to me?

We were on the towpath by the Tiber.

You said, 'I can't go on. I'm done for. My sins are eating me away, like wood riddled by woodworm.'

'Take heart,' I said. 'If you want to win through, you only have to believe.'

Didn't Jesus say, 'Make no doubt about it, if your faith is the size of a mustard seed, say to this mountain, move away, and it will move'? (Matt. 17:20).

Your own mountain to be moved was the chain that bound you and paralysed your will.

Remember?

What happened, Leonard?

Did you see the Dead Sea divide?

Did you see the walls of Jericho fall down?

We who fought at Jericho.

Many, many a battle I've seen at Jericho.

Remember, Lucy? You were as good as dead.

There didn't seem a breath of life in you.

Your whole world had fallen in.

But you had what it took to escape from the morass, one spring like a panther's and that was enough.

And you found yourself with victory in your fist.

What joy to look down from the walls and contemplate the marvels that the Lord has wrought in you.

We who have fought at Jericho.

Remember, brothers and sisters engaged on the Neo-Catechumenal Way?

Do you remember that day, that moment?

You've told me yourselves in richly joyful song about your victory over those walls:

Say to the faint-hearted,
Say it, say it to the poor:
'Be strong, don't be afraid . . .
Your God is coming to save you.' (cf. Isa. 35:4)

And not only the walls collapsed.

Non-faith collapsed, non-hope collapsed.

God was there and you saw.

As Isaiah said long ago:

Then the eyes of the blind will be opened,
the ears of the deaf unsealed,
then the lame will leap like a deer
and the tongues of the dumb sing for joy. (Isa. 35:5–6)

We who fought at Jericho.
Remember, you who seek to renew yourselves in the Spirit?
Remember!
We held up our arms day and night, we shouted, we wept and then we witnessed the miracle.
The walls fell down and Jericho was ours.
Ours the Jericho of prayer, the Jericho of intercession, the Jericho of contemplation.
Now it's worthwhile being alive.
Before, it wasn't.
Now at last we feel free, masters of ourselves and of our land.
God, my God!
How great you are!

I want to remember Harry too; I want to remember you as well, George, Joan, Stephen, Thomas, Mary, Louise, Samantha, Dianne.
Tell us, tell what you saw at Jericho.
Tell what happened.
One step was enough, one shout was enough, a nothing was enough and everything was achieved.
Joe, do you remember the day?
When you came to me weighed down with defeat and sickened by your cowardly behaviour.
Tell us, tell us now, Joe.
You rose to your feet like a lion, you shouted your 'I will, Lord,' you believed in the possibility of seeing the sun rise, you put your trust in God, you flung yourself into hope.
You won, Joe. Truer still, God won in you.
Now you have peace of mind, now you know what you want to do; tomorrow doesn't frighten you any more.
With him beside you, you can go up to the battle.

You, having fought at Jericho, have triumphed.

And wasn't it easy!
  Say so, tell the poor: it was perfectly easy.
  It was enough not to believe in oneself, not to trust in oneself.
  It was enough to escape from self in the dark night and fly like a mad thing towards the light of dawn.
  It was enough to give up one's idols.
  They were a delusion.

'They had hands but couldn't touch,
they had feet but couldn't walk,
they had throats but couldn't sing.' (cf. Ps. 115)

They were idols made of wood or silver, not of flesh.
Whereas God was the valiant, living, invincible One.
He wanted so little of us
And yet it seemed so hard.
Non-faith, non-hope, non-love – all delusions!
Now we have overcome.
We who fought at Jericho.

11

'O Glorious Cross of
the Risen Lord'

And now we come to the end of the journey: the cross.

Further than this we cannot go . . . and here for ever I can stay.

There is no higher hill than Calvary.

Once I have given my all, there's nothing left for me to do but ratify my self-giving beside the tree of eternal life, in whose shadow I have pitched my tent and from whose roots I still draw nourishment.

Going my journey to the infinite, I can still march on, without moving, awestruck in contemplation.

This is true possession of the kingdom.

At my exodus I started out to free myself from slavery, I purified myself in the desert, I crossed the cloud of divine unknowing, I saw the kingdom and acquired it like a treasure hidden in a field, I hoped against all hope, I consented to have faith, I fought at Jericho.

That left me this final step, beyond faith itself, and now I confront God's greatest revelation in Jesus.

We must strain every aspect of our being to seize the absolute revelation.

Some time had passed since that memorable night in the cathedral when – accidentally, as it seemed – I'd attended the assembly at Shechem of all the foetuses and embryos conceived and aborted in the great modern city.

That night the unborn babies had appeared to me in visible form as angels, archangels, cherubim and seraphim, and I had, in that vast cathedral, listened to their words and little voices, which were very far from sad.

The memory of it was so sharp to me that I wanted to have another look, hard as that would probably be.

Who could tell where they had got to by now?

Who could tell what point on their journey they'd reached?

It wouldn't do any harm to try, I thought. Moved by curiosity and high hope, I went back to the city.

As on the first occasion, I got myself locked inside the cathedral by using the same ruse as before.

The sacristan seemed particularly well disposed towards me.

He told me his asthma was a great deal better and that his son – wasn't this a miracle! – had now got a job in Crédit Suisse.

All this, strangely enough, he attributed to my prayers.

I went back to the same seat in the choir-stalls and found everything looking just as before.

The lamp before the sacrament glowed red: an effect produced by a kind of night-light sold in large quantities in town for putting on the graves in the city cemetery.

Everything was quiet.

It wasn't as cold as it had been on my first visit and, being tired, I had to make quite an effort not to fall asleep.

When the little angels began assembling, I was wide awake.

I was determined not to miss a second opportunity of seeing what had made such a deep impression on me the first time that I hadn't been able to get it out of my head.

From the instant the angels started arriving, I observed they were much livelier, more alert and full of personality.

In no time the cathedral was crowded to an unbelievable degree.

To find room for themselves, many had to perch inside the confessional boxes and a huge number invaded the sacristy, where they quickly set up closed-circuit TV. The light emanating from the cherubim was beautiful to see and although the cathedral lights were out there was no need for them.

When the angels had all taken up their posts, a great silence
fell.

All turned towards the high altar which was as big as the
one in St Peter's, Rome.

In the pulpit, behind the reading desk, stood a cherub who
was to act as reader.

Wearing a red dalmatic, he had the Bible open before him
at the fifth chapter of the Book of Revelation.

I was doing my best to concentrate when the beating of
wings very close to me distracted me somewhat.

My former friend, whom the hospital orderly and I had
discovered as an abortion in the hospital rubbish-skip, had
landed on my knee as before.

It was undoubtedly he, but in much better health and
remarkably cheerful.

He told me he was very pleased to see me, that there were
many things he wanted to tell me and that he now had a
name: Isaac.

'I'll explain to you later.'

Meanwhile he'd taken up his usual position on the knee I
always keep crossed, since in that position my leg doesn't
hurt so much.

The reader had started reading his passage from the Apocalypse and the cathedral was silent as the grave.

'Do not weep;
the Lion of the Tribe of Judah,
the Root of David, has triumphed,
so he will open the book and its seven seals.'
Then I saw in the middle of the throne
with its four living creatures and the circle of elders
a Lamb that seemed to have been sacrificed.
It had seven horns and seven eyes,
which are the seven Spirits
that God has sent out over the whole world.
And the Lamb came forward and took the scroll
from the right hand of the One sitting on the throne.
And when he took it,
the four living creatures prostrated themselves before him

and with them the twenty-four elders,
each of them holding a harp
and a golden bowl full of incense
which are the prayers of the saints.
They sang a new hymn:
'You are worthy to take the scroll
and to break its seals
because you were sacrificed
and with your blood bought people for God
of every race, language, people and nation,
and made them a line of kings and priests for God,
to rule the world.' (Rev. 5:5–10)

When the first reading was over, all fell into deep meditation.

I felt so happy.

I was completely caught up in that heavenly assembly described in the reading, for it told of one of the final stages of the journey, perhaps the last of all.

For its central theme was the sacrificed Lamb, Jesus of Nazareth.

Little Isaac, perching on my knee, leaned closer towards me, so as not to cause a disturbance, and said, 'You know, Carlo, I offered my life for my mother and a marvellous thing came about: she's turned to the Lord.

'But that's not all: she's remembered me and given me a name: "The child I murdered before he was born, I name him Isaac."

'A fine name. I like it.

'They've informed the registrar about me.

'Now everything's OK and my papers are in order.

'I'm called Isaac.

'And my mother now lives like a saint.

'I prayed for her a great deal on my journey, but grace only seized on her when I offered my life for her sake.

'I guess this must be the golden rule up here.

'In any case, it *can* only be like that, once we begin adoring the Lamb who was sacrificed for all.'

Isaac laughed with his hand over his mouth, so as not to make a noise.

'I can't tell you how my mother cries whenever she thinks of me!

'She cries and she prays.

'I'm very fond of her and hope I'll be able to appear to her soon.

'But it isn't the moment yet; that's for the Spirit to decide.'

I asked Isaac what he was doing now.

He said, 'We have to go on praying.

'We've come to adore the cross.

'It's the last stage of the journey.

'Listen.

'One of our girl-readers will be reading the next lesson.

'She's called Sarah. She was a famous abortion in her time.

'She was murdered in her sixth month. What a bloodbath!

'But her father was the guilty one; he didn't want her.

'He was a doctor and forced Sarah's mother to have an abortion.

'Poor little woman, she suffered dreadfully.

'Sarah's been praying for her like anything and offered her life for her, just like me.

'She offered her life for her father too, even though he'd been so selfish and overbearing, but now he's got the message.

'Just imagine! Husband and wife have made a clean break with the past and gone off to live with the lepers in Africa, he as a doctor and she as a nurse!

'How great the power of love is, Carlo! Through love, God can turn even the hardest hearts!

'We ought to feel very sorry for human beings.

'They do all these terrible things because they don't understand what they're doing.'

Meanwhile Sarah had flitted into the pulpit and in her piping voice began the second reading. In point of fact she sang it, accompanying herself on a tiny harp. It was the hymn of the cross.

O glorious cross of the risen Lord,
O tree of my salvation!
On it I feed, in it is my delight;
in its roots I grow,
in its branches I expand.
Its dew fills me with joy,
its breeze makes me fruitful,
I have pitched my tent in its shade.
In hunger sustenance,
in thirst a living spring,
clothing in nakedness.
Royal road, my narrow way,
Jacob's ladder, couch of love
where the Lord has wedded me.
In fear a defence,
in stumbling a support,
in victory the crown,
in the struggle, you the reward.
Tree of eternal life,
pillar of the universe,
framework of the earth,
your head touches Heaven
and in your open arms
shines forth the love of God.
                (from An Easter Homily by Ippolito Romano)

When Sarah had finished singing the second reading, there
was a long pause for meditation.

Those angels coming from the desert were used to silence
and obviously loved practising it after hearing the word of
God read aloud or sung.

It was an impressive sight and I was glad the night was
still young so that I could enjoy the service of adoration of
the cross in peace.

Next spoke up an archangel, who seemed to enjoy great
prestige among those present.

'In Exodus,' he said, 'there is a story about mysterious
serpents which bit the Israelites, causing them to die.

'Many died and the people of God suffered in consequence.

'But at this point the story becomes a beautiful allegory, telling of One who turns into a serpent with power to save those who raise their eyes to it.

'We know who the image of the brazen serpent alludes to, with its power of setting those free who look at it.

'It's a prophetic vision of Christ, appearing in his saving might on the cross.

'But in order to save, he lets himself be impaled and raised aloft, and in order to heal, he asks us to look at him, if we are to fully grasp the meaning of his saving act and imitate it.

'To look at him will be enough.

'And what do I see when I look at him, what do I gather from his mysterious act?

'This: that I can achieve total identity with him who, with total acceptance, has submitted himself to this.

'By this act of identity, he consented to be "serpent" in all things like every other "serpent", except in sin.

'Herein lies the secret of everything, herein lies the power to break death's vicious circle and to discover the revelation of God's love.

'Jesus consented to become "sin", consented to the greatest humiliation possible for God's holiness, "becoming serpent" to save his brother- and sister-serpents.

'What a distance lies between the love shown by God in becoming human to save the human race, and the justice of the Old Law which, while imposing an unbearable burden on the human race, was still unable to save it.

'What an abyss in this infinite humiliation, this radical self-abasement of God's holiness, choosing to die for love rather than defend himself by force of justice and the law.

'Jesus became "serpent" and, undergoing the ultimate humiliation, identified himself completely with the race of serpents known as human beings.

'And lest we should think this sign given us in the desert was in any way accidental, Christ hews to the same line, clinching his total identification at the Jordan.

'Once past the sand, the rocks, the desert and having

reached the liberating waters of purification, he asks John to baptise him.

'And in answer to John's objection: "That can't be. You are the holy one, you should baptise me" (cf. Matt. 3:14), he resists and, faithful to his own teaching, compels John to baptise him, once again showing his thirst for total identity with sinners.

'But that's not all.

'There is the final act, outdoing anything that might have been foreseen: as powerful as a heavenly symphony.

'I mean, the final act on Calvary.

'As though in some strange and beautiful icon, Jesus hangs on the cross.

'Beside him, to left and right, two thieves, sentenced for various crimes.

'One of them sets himself up as judge and, resentfully, rabidly insults Jesus without any justification, saying:

'"Aren't you the Christ? Save yourself and us as well."

'But the other one reproves him:

'"Have you no fear of God at all? You got the same sentence as he did, but in our case we deserved it: we are paying for what we did. But this man has done nothing wrong."

'And adds, with supreme poetry:

'"Jesus, remember me when you come into your kingdom."

'To which comes the reply, the divine reply going beyond all bounds of time and space:

'"In truth I tell you, today you will be with me in paradise"' (Luke 23:39–43).

Who could have imagined such a thing?

To whom could so sublime a mystery have been revealed?

I was open-mouthed at the maturity of the angel who had been speaking.

I could see the assembly appreciated the sermon too.

What astonished me was the exultant joy with which they heard the Word.

None of them was thinking about the past; none of them harboured rancour or regret.

And when you consider they were a murdered nation, a people who had come out of great tribulation, as the Apocalypse says, a people massacred by human wickedness and thoughtlessness . . .

None of these little ones demanded justice.

All of them, I think, like Isaac and Sarah, had offered their lives for those who had murdered them.

On the altar stood the Blessed Sacrament, the sign of the sacrificed Lamb.

Then I understood.

Then I understood.

Then I understood.

The law didn't matter.

Crime didn't matter.

Human wickedness didn't matter.

What mattered was the humility of the sacrificed Lamb.

The blood didn't matter.

Even the cross didn't matter, although so many of them, like Christ, had been crucified.

What mattered was forgiveness.

What mattered was being able to reconcile and be reconciled.

That is the apex of the journey.

The apex for Jesus, and for us who look to Jesus.

The summit of the journey is forgiveness.

As I looked at the assembly in the cathedral I realised all these 'little martyrs' had forgiven everyone.

Not only that.

They loved those who had done them wrong.

They had offered their lives for them.

Now peace was possible, truly possible.

If at that moment all the women who had debased themselves by murdering their children in the womb had entered the cathedral in procession, these little creatures would have taken off from the picture-frames, the lamps, the vaulting, the cornices and flown to find their mothers – much as lambs when the ewes appear – and hugged them as no one had ever attempted to hug them before.

No wonder the Church so madly shouts *Exultet.*

O happy guilt!

O happy guilt!

O happy guilt!

Now I understand, now I see.

Sin hadn't succeeded in dividing these families but in binding them tighter under the cloak of compassion.

These children loved their mothers more perhaps than those who had received a loving upbringing.

O mystery of the human heart!

O mystery of Christ crucified!

O mystery of forgiveness!

I was tired after such an intense and profoundly moving experience.

Before dropping off peacefully to sleep in my choir-stall, I asked Isaac: 'In your view, is the journey long or short?'

I told him that, thanks to my perfectionist obsessions, I had always imagined purgatory must be incredibly long, lasting from age to geological age.

'What do you think about this?'

In his clear little voice, Isaac replied:

'What does Luke say when recounting what Jesus said to the thief on the cross?

'"Today, today you will be with me in paradise."'

Today.

Today.

Today!

It took a little aborted child to make me grasp what I had never succeeded in grasping in spite of all my years and philosophy.

Yes, today.

And I fell asleep in peace.

Little Isaac amused himself for a while by calling me to order with flicks of his tiny wings, since I was snoring and disturbing the assembly now in peaceful, silent meditation on the mystery of forgiveness.

Prayers to Help on the March

**A Little Guide for
Six Days of Prayer
with the Word of God**

It seems right to end this book about the 'journey' by inviting the reader to pray.

It's never a mistake to pray and I'm convinced that nothing can resist the power of prayer.

The prayers are arranged as short offices to be said either alone or in community, like morning and evening prayer.

The subject for the day will be found in the appropriate chapter of the book, as indicated. The office begins with a psalm and then the scriptural reading is indicated.

First Day
Monday

*And God
created
heaven and earth.* (Gen. 1:1)

MORNING: Hope (see Introduction)

Psalm 84: How blessed are those who live in your house:
they shall praise you continually.

How lovely are your dwelling-places,
   Yahweh Sabaoth.
My whole being yearns and pines
   for Yahweh's courts,
My heart and my body cry out for joy
   to the living God.

Even the sparrow has found a home,
the swallow a nest to place its young:
your altars, Yahweh Sabaoth,
   my King and my God.

How blessed are those who live in your house;
   they shall praise you continually.
Blessed those who find their strength in you,
   whose hearts are set on pilgrimage.

As they pass through the Valley of the Balsam,
they make there a water-hole,
and – a further blessing – early rain fills it.
They make their way from height to height,
God shows himself to them in Zion.

Yahweh, God Sabaoth, hear my prayer,
listen, God of Jacob.
God, our shield, look,
and see the face of your anointed.

Better one day in your courts
    than a thousand at my own devices,
to stand on the threshold of God's house
    than to live in the tents of the wicked.

For Yahweh God is a rampart and shield,
    he gives grace and glory;
Yahweh refuses nothing good
    to those whose life is blameless.

Yahweh Sabaoth,
    blessed is he who trusts in you.

READING: Ephesians (entire).

EVENING: The Creation (see Chapter 1)

Psalm 104: The earth is full
              of your creatures.

Bless Yahweh, my soul,
Yahweh, my God, how great you are!
Clothed in majesty and splendour,
wearing the light as a robe!

You stretch out the heavens like a tent,
build your palace on the waters above,
making the clouds your chariot,
gliding on the wings of the wind,
appointing the winds your messengers,
flames of fire your servants.

You fixed the earth on its foundations,
for ever and ever it shall not be shaken;
you covered it with the deep like a garment,
the waters overtopping the mountains.

At your reproof the waters fled,
at the voice of your thunder they sped away,
flowing over mountains, down valleys,
to the place you had fixed for them;
you made a limit they were not to cross,
they were not to return and cover the earth.

In the ravines you opened up springs,
running down between the mountains,
supplying water for all the wild beasts;
the wild asses quench their thirst,
on their banks the birds of the air make their nests,
they sing among the leaves.

From your high halls you water the mountains,
satisfying the earth with the fruit of your works:
for cattle you make the grass grow,
and for people the plants they need,

to bring forth food from the earth,
and wine to cheer people's hearts,
oil to make their faces glow,
food to make them sturdy of heart.

The trees of Yahweh drink their fill,
the cedars of Lebanon which he sowed;
there the birds build their nests,
on the highest branches the stork makes its home;
for the wild goats there are the mountains,
in the crags the coneys find refuge.

He made the moon to mark the seasons,
the sun knows when to set.
You bring on darkness, and night falls,
when all the forest beasts roam around;
young lions roar for their prey,
asking God for their food.

The sun rises and away they steal,
back to their lairs to lie down,
and man goes out to work,
to labour till evening falls.

How countless are your works, Yahweh,
all of them made so wisely!
The earth is full of your creatures.

Then there is the sea, with its vast expanses
teeming with countless creatures,
creatures both great and small;
there ships pass to and fro,
and Leviathan whom you made to sport with.

They all depend upon you,
to feed them when they need it.
You provide the food they gather,
your open hand gives them their fill.

Turn away your face and they panic;
take back their breath and they die
and revert to dust.
Send out your breath and life begins;
you renew the face of the earth.

Glory to Yahweh for ever!
May Yahweh find joy in his creatures!
At his glance the earth trembles,
at his touch the mountains pour forth smoke.

I shall sing to Yahweh all my life,
make music for my God as long as I live.
May my musings be pleasing to him,
for Yahweh gives me joy.

READING: Genesis 1 and 2.

Second Day
Tuesday

On my back
ploughmen have set to work
making long furrows. (Ps. 129:3)

MORNING: Evil (see Chapter 2)

Psalm 14: When Yahweh brings his people home.

The fool has said in his heart,
    'There is no God.'
Their deeds are corrupt and vile,
    not one of them does right.

Yahweh looks down from heaven
    at the children of Adam.
To see if a single one is wise,
    a single one seeks God.

All have turned away,
    all alike turned sour,
not one of them does right,
    not a single one.

Are they not aware, all these evil-doers?
    They are devouring my people,
    this is the bread they eat,
    and they never call to Yahweh.

They will be gripped with fear,
    where there is no need for fear,
for God takes the side of the upright;
    you may mock the plans of the poor,

but Yahweh is their refuge.

Who will bring from Zion salvation for Israel?
When Yahweh brings his people home,
what joy for Jacob, what happiness for Israel!

READING: Genesis 38.

EVENING: The new assembly at Shechem (see Chapter 3)

Psalm 124:   Then water was washing us away.

If Yahweh had not been on our side
   – let Israel repeat it –
if Yahweh had not been on our side
   when people attacked us,
they would have swallowed us alive
   in the heat of their anger.

Then water was washing us away,
   a torrent running right over us;
running right over us then
   were turbulent waters.

Blessed be Yahweh for not letting us fall
   a prey to their teeth!
We escaped like a bird
   from the fowlers' net.

The net was broken
   and we escaped;
our help is in the name of Yahweh,
   who made heaven and earth.

READING: Joshua 24.

Third Day
Wednesday

Come
come with me
into the desert
I shall talk to you of love
heart to heart. (Hosea)

MORNING: The exodus (see Chapter 4)

Psalm 126:   . . . bringing in his sheaves.

When Yahweh brought back Zion's captives
   we lived in a dream;
then our mouths filled with laughter,
   and our lips with song.

Then the nations kept saying, 'What great deeds
   Yahweh has done for them!'
Yes, Yahweh did great deeds for us,
   and we were overjoyed.

Bring back, Yahweh, our people from captivity
   like torrents in the Negeb!
Those who sow in tears
   sing as they reap.

He went off, went off weeping,
   carrying the seed.
He comes back, comes back singing,
   bringing in his sheaves.

READING: Deuteronomy 1–6.

EVENING: The desert (see Chapter 5)

Psalm 136:   His faithful love endures for ever.

Give thanks to Yahweh for he is good,
for his faithful love endures for ever.
Give thanks to the God of gods,
for his faithful love endures for ever.
Give thanks to the Lord of lords,
for his faithful love endures for ever.

He alone works wonders,
for his faithful love endures for ever.
In wisdom he made the heavens,
for his faithful love endures for ever.
He set the earth firm on the waters,
for his faithful love endures for ever.

He made the great lights,
for his faithful love endures for ever.
The sun to rule the day,
for his faithful love endures for ever.
Moon and stars to rule the night,
for his faithful love endures for ever.

He struck down the first-born of Egypt,
for his faithful love endures for ever.
He brought Israel out from among them,
for his faithful love endures for ever.
With mighty hand and outstretched arm,
for his faithful love endures for ever.

He split the Sea of Reeds in two,
for his faithful love endures for ever,
Let Israel pass through the middle,
for his faithful love endures for ever.
And drowned Pharaoh and all his army,
for his faithful love endures for ever.

He led his people through the desert,
for his faithful love endures for ever.

He struck down mighty kings,
for his faithful love endures for ever.
Slaughtered famous kings,
for his faithful love endures for ever.
Sihon king of the Amorites,
for his faithful love endures for ever.
And Og king of Bashan,
for his faithful love endures for ever.

He gave their land as a birthright,
for his faithful love endures for ever.
A birthright to his servant Israel,
for his faithful love endures for ever.
He kept us in mind when we were humbled,
for his faithful love endures for ever.
And rescued us from our enemies,
for his faithful love endures for ever.

He provides food for all living creatures,
for his faithful love endures for ever.
Give thanks to the God of heaven,
for his faithful love endures for ever.

READING: Hosea (entire).

Fourth Day
Thursday

The kingdom
of heaven
is like
a treasure hidden
in a field. (Matt. 13:44)

MORNING: The dark night (see Chapter 6)

Psalm 88:   Why, Yahweh, do you turn your face away from
            me?

Yahweh, God of my salvation,
when I cry out to you in the night,
may my prayer reach your presence,
hear my cry for help.

For I am filled with misery,
my life is on the brink of Sheol;
already numbered among those who sink into oblivion,
I am as one bereft of strength,

left alone among the dead,
like the slaughtered lying in the grave,
whom you remember no more,
cut off as they are from your protection.

You have plunged me to the bottom of the grave,
in the darkness, in the depths;
weighted down by your anger,
kept low by your waves.

You have deprived me of my friends,

made me repulsive to them,
imprisoned, with no escape;
my eyes are worn out with suffering.
I call to you, Yahweh, all day,
I stretch out my hands to you.

Do you work wonders for the dead,
can shadows rise up to praise you?
Do they speak in the grave of your faithful love,
of your constancy in the place of perdition?
Are your wonders known in the darkness,
your saving justice in the land of oblivion?

But, for my part, I cry to you, Yahweh,
every morning my prayer comes before you;
why, Yahweh, do you rebuff me,
turn your face away from me?

Wretched and close to death since childhood,
I have borne your terrors – I am finished!
Your anger has overwhelmed me,
your terrors annihilated me.

They flood around me all day long,
close in on me all at once.
You have deprived me of friends and companions,
and all that I know is the dark.

READING: Luke 22 and 23.

EVENING: The kingdom (see Chapter 7)

Psalm 72:   He rescues anyone needy who calls to him.

God, endow the king with your own fair judgement,
    the son of the king with your own saving justice,
that he may rule your people with justice,
    and your poor with fair judgement.

Mountains and hills,
    bring peace to the people!

With justice he will judge the poor of the people,
he will save the children of the needy
   and crush their oppressors.

In the sight of the sun and the moon he will endure,
   age after age.
He will come down like rain on mown grass,
   like showers moistening the land:

In his days uprightness shall flourish,
   and peace in plenty till the moon is no more.
His empire shall stretch from sea to sea,
   from the river to the limits of the earth.

The Beast will cower before him,
   his enemies lick the dust;
the kings of Tarshish and the islands
   will pay him tribute.

The kings of Sheba and Saba
   will offer gifts;
all kings will do him homage,
   all nations become his servants.

For he rescues anyone needy who calls to him,
   and the poor who has no one to help.
He has pity on the weak and the needy,
   and saves the needy from death.

From oppression and violence he redeems their lives,
   their blood is precious in his sight.
Long may he live; may the gold of Sheba be given him!
Prayer will be offered for him constantly,
   and blessings invoked on him all day.

May wheat abound in the land,
   waving on the heights of the hills,
like Lebanon with its fruits and flowers at their best,
   like ˋhe grasses of the earth.

May his name be blessed for ever,
   and endure in the sight of the sun.
In him shall be blessed every race in the world,

and all nations call him blessed.

Blessed be Yahweh, the God of Israel,
  who alone works wonders;
blessed for ever his glorious name.
May the whole world be filled with his glory!
  Amen! Amen!

READING: Revelation 21 and 22.

Fifth Day
Friday

Whoever trusts
in the Lord
is like Mount Zion. (Ps. 125:1)

MORNING: God, you are my God (see Chapter 8)

Psalm 63:   My heart thirsts for you.

God, you are my God, I pine for you;
my heart thirsts for you,
my body longs for you,
as a land parched, dreary and waterless.
Thus I have gazed on you in the sanctuary,
seeing your power and your glory.

Better your faithful love than life itself;
my lips will praise you.
Thus I will bless you all my life,
in your name lift up my hands.
All my longings fulfilled as with fat and rich foods,
a song of joy on my lips and praise in my mouth.

On my bed when I think of you,
I muse on you in the watches of the night,
for you have always been my help;
in the shadow of your wings I rejoice;
my heart clings to you;
your right hand supports me.

READING: Tobit (entire).

EVENING: The God of the impossible (see Chapter 9)

Psalm 62: In God alone.

In God alone there is rest for my soul,
    from him comes my safety;
he alone is my rock, my safety,
    my stronghold so that I stand unshaken.

How much longer will you set on a victim,
    all together, intent on murder,
like a rampart already leaning over,
    a wall already damaged?
Trickery is their only plan,
    deception their only pleasure,
with lies on their lips they pronounce a blessing,
    with a curse in their hearts.

Rest in God alone, my soul!
    He is the source of my hope.
He alone is my rock, my safety,
    my stronghold, so that I stand unwavering.
In God is my safety and my glory,
    the rock of my strength.

In God is my refuge; trust in him,
    you people, at all times.
Pour out your hearts to him,
    God is a refuge for us.

Ordinary people are a mere puff of wind,
    important people a delusion;
set both on the scales together,
    and they are lighter than a puff of wind.
Put no trust in extortion,
    no empty hopes in robbery;
however much wealth may multiply,
    do not set your heart on it.

Once God has spoken,
    twice have I heard this:

Strength belongs to God,
   to you, Lord, faithful love;
   and you repay everyone as their deeds deserve.

READING: Daniel 13.

Sixth Day
Saturday

O glorious cross of the risen Lord,
O tree of my salvation!
On it I feed, in it is my delight;
in its roots I grow,
in its branches I expand.

Tree of eternal life,
pillar of the universe,
framework of the earth,
your head touches Heaven
and in your open arms
shines forth the love of God.
                    (from An Easter Homily by Ippolito Romano)

MORNING: We who fought at Jericho (see Chapter 10)

Psalm 31:   When I cried out to you.

In you, Yahweh, I have taken refuge,
let me never be put to shame,
in your saving justice deliver me, rescue me,
turn your ear to me, make haste.

Be for me a rock-fastness,
a fortified citadel to save me.
You are my rock, my rampart;
true to your name, lead me and guide me!

Draw me out of the net they have spread for me,
for you are my refuge;
to your hands I commit my spirit,
by you have I been redeemed.

God of truth, you hate
worshippers of ineffectual idols;
but my trust is in Yahweh:
I will delight and rejoice in your faithful love!

You, who have seen my misery
and witnessed the miseries of my soul,
have not handed me over to the enemy,
but have given me freedom to roam at large.

Take pity on me, Yahweh,
   for I am in trouble.
Vexation is gnawing away my eyes,
   my soul deep within me.

For my life is worn out with sorrow,
   and my years with sighs.
My strength gives way under my misery,
   and my bones are all wasted away.

The sheer number of my enemies
   makes me contemptible,
loathsome to my neighbours,
   and my friends shrink from me in horror.

When people see me in the street
   they take to their heels.
I have no more place in their hearts than a corpse,
   or something lost.

All I hear is slander
   – terror wherever I turn –
as they plot together against me,
   scheming to take my life.

But my trust is in you, Yahweh;
   I say, 'You are my God,'
every moment of my life is in your hands, rescue me
   from the clutches of my foes who pursue me;
let your face shine on your servant,
   save me in your faithful love.

READING: Joshua 6:1–16.

EVENING: This is the Passover of the Lord (see Chapter 11)

Psalm 30: You have turned my mourning into dancing.

I praise you to the heights, Yahweh, for you have raised me
    up,
you have not let my foes make merry over me.
Yahweh, my God, I cried to you for help and you healed
    me.
Yahweh, you have lifted me out of Sheol,
from among those who sink into oblivion you have given me
    life.

Make music for Yahweh, all you who are faithful to him,
praise his unforgettable holiness.
His anger lasts but a moment, his favour through life;
In the evening come tears, but with dawn cries of joy.

    Carefree, I used to think,
    'Nothing can ever shake me!'
Your favour, Yahweh, set me on unassailable heights,
but you turned away your face and I was terrified.

    To you, Yahweh, I call,
    to my God I cry for mercy.
What point is there in my death, my going down to the
    abyss?
Can the dust praise you or proclaim your faithfulness?

Listen, Yahweh, take pity on me,
    Yahweh, be my help!
You have turned my mourning into dancing,
you have stripped off my sackcloth and clothed me with joy.
So my heart will sing to you unceasingly,
Yahweh, my God, I shall praise you for ever.

READING: Luke 23 and 24.